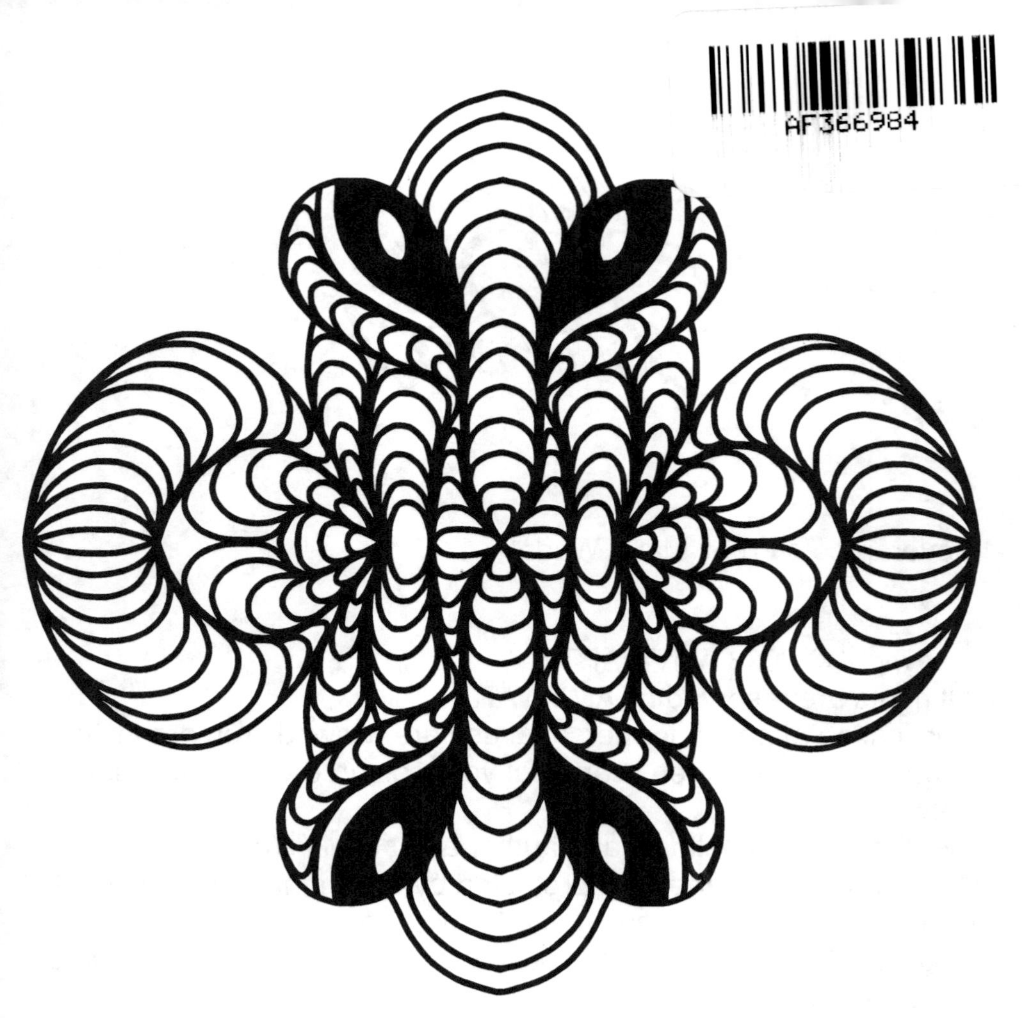

ABSTRACT COLORING 4
COLORING FOR ALL
BY
MARIA WEDEL

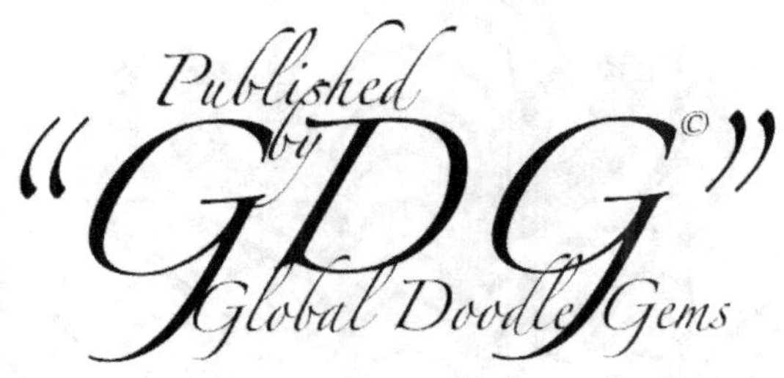

Coverart colored by Maria Wedel

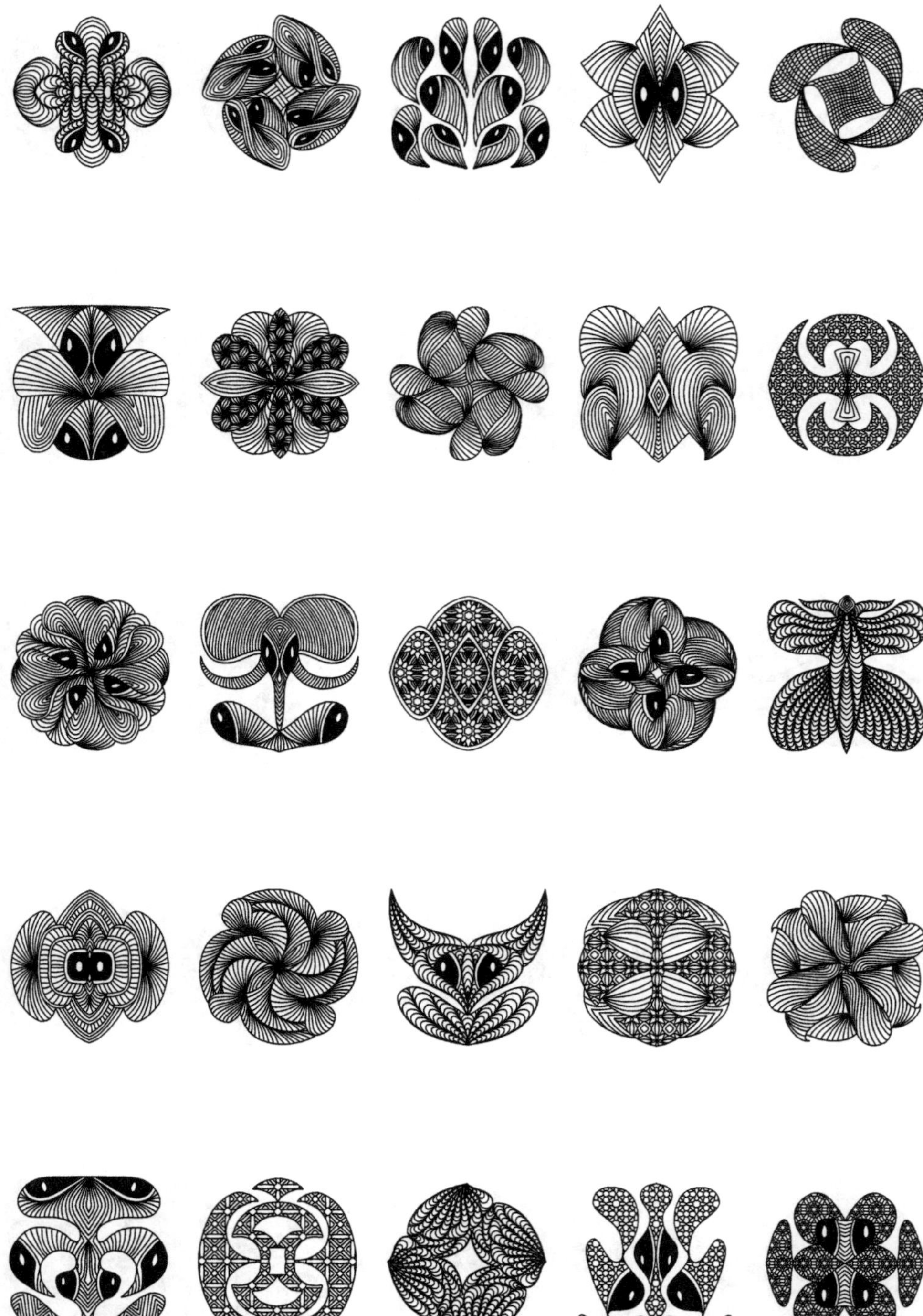

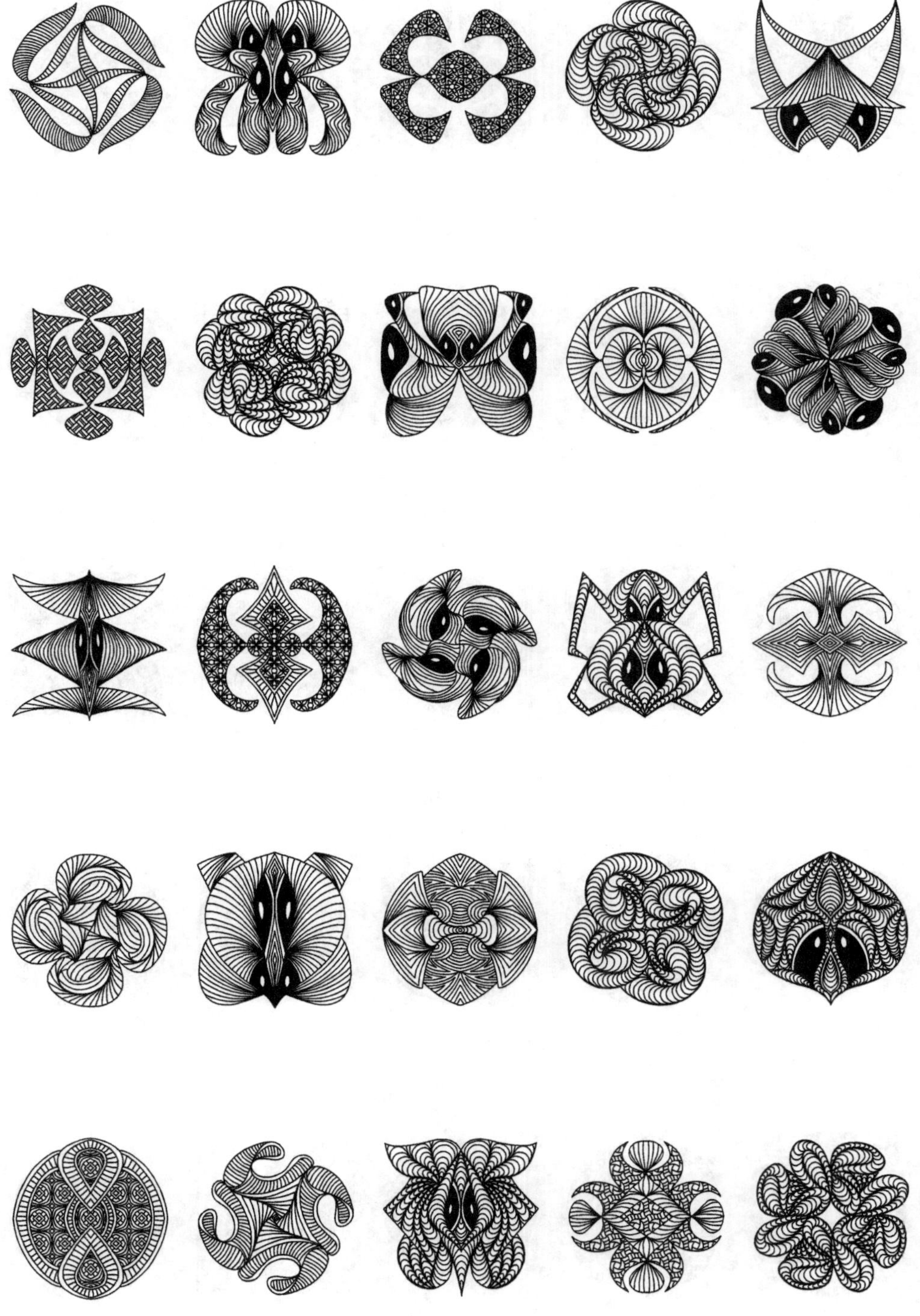

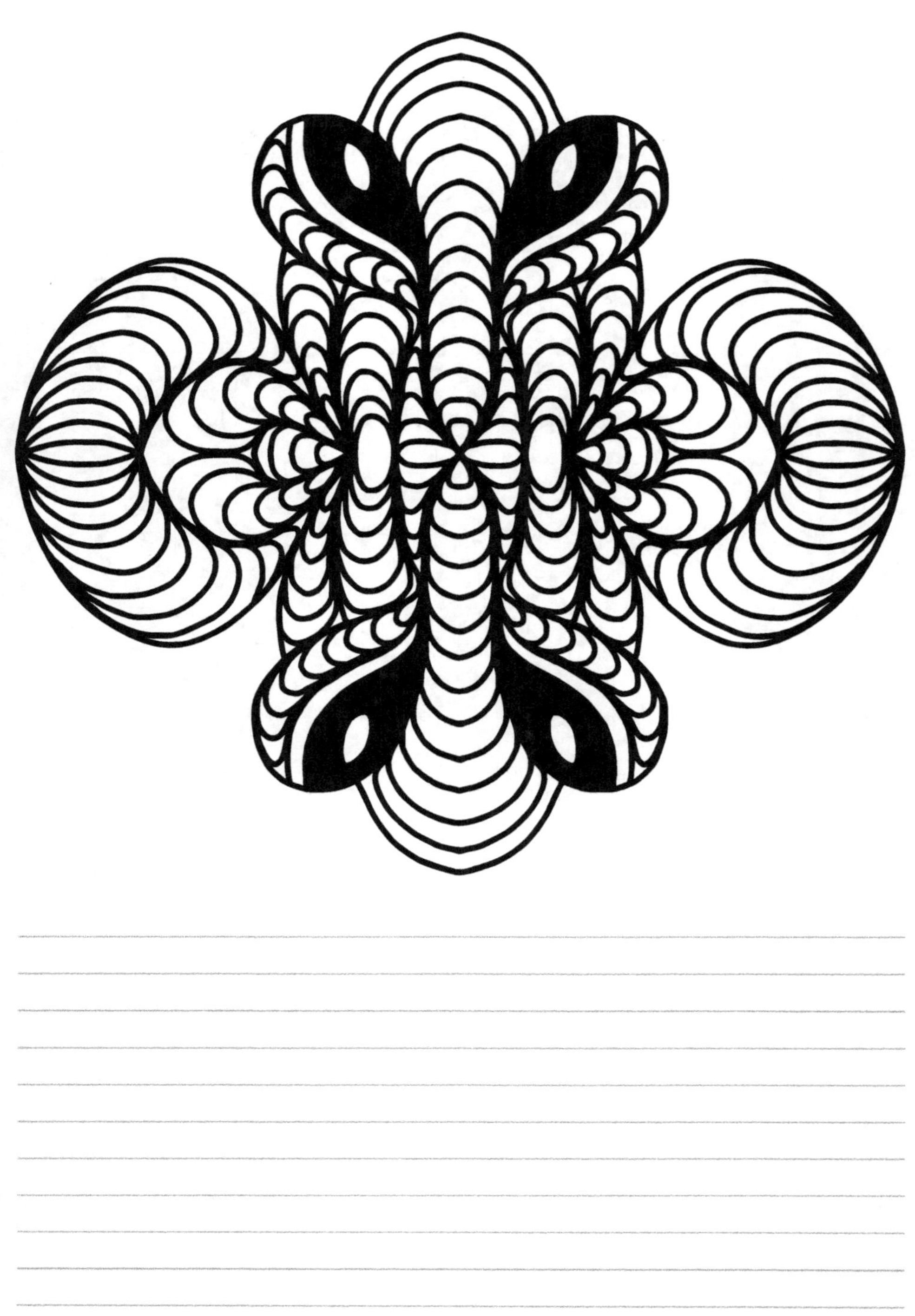

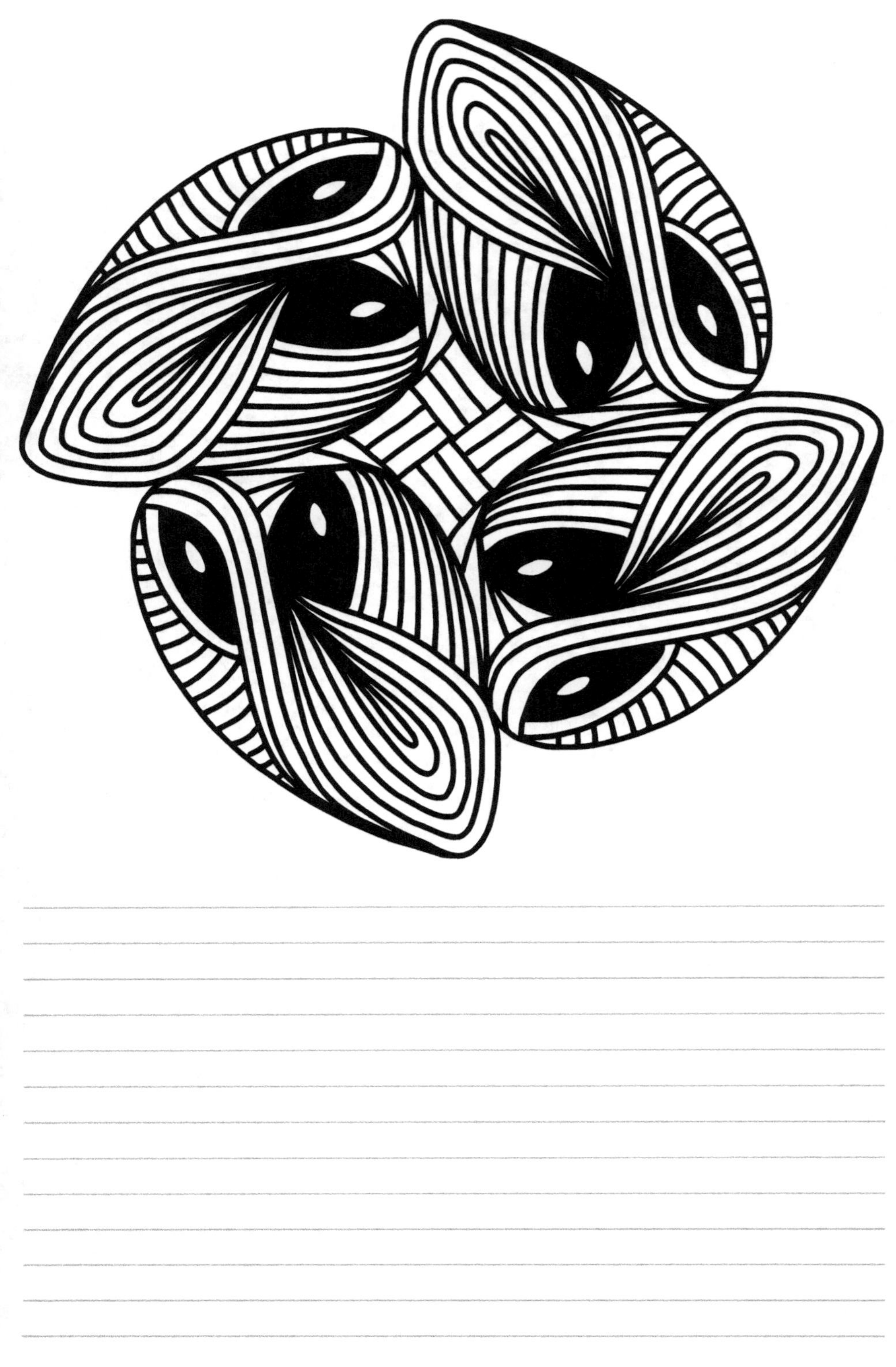

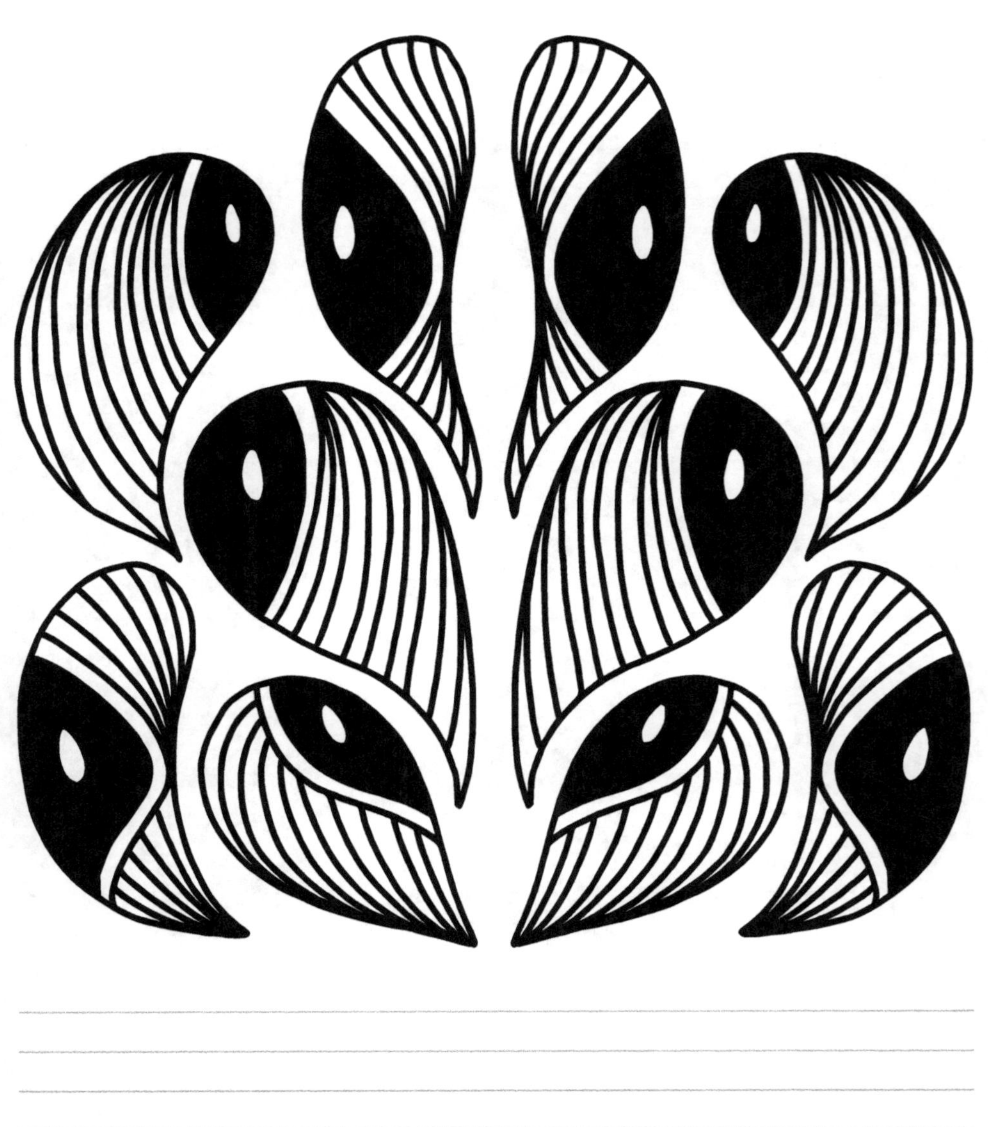

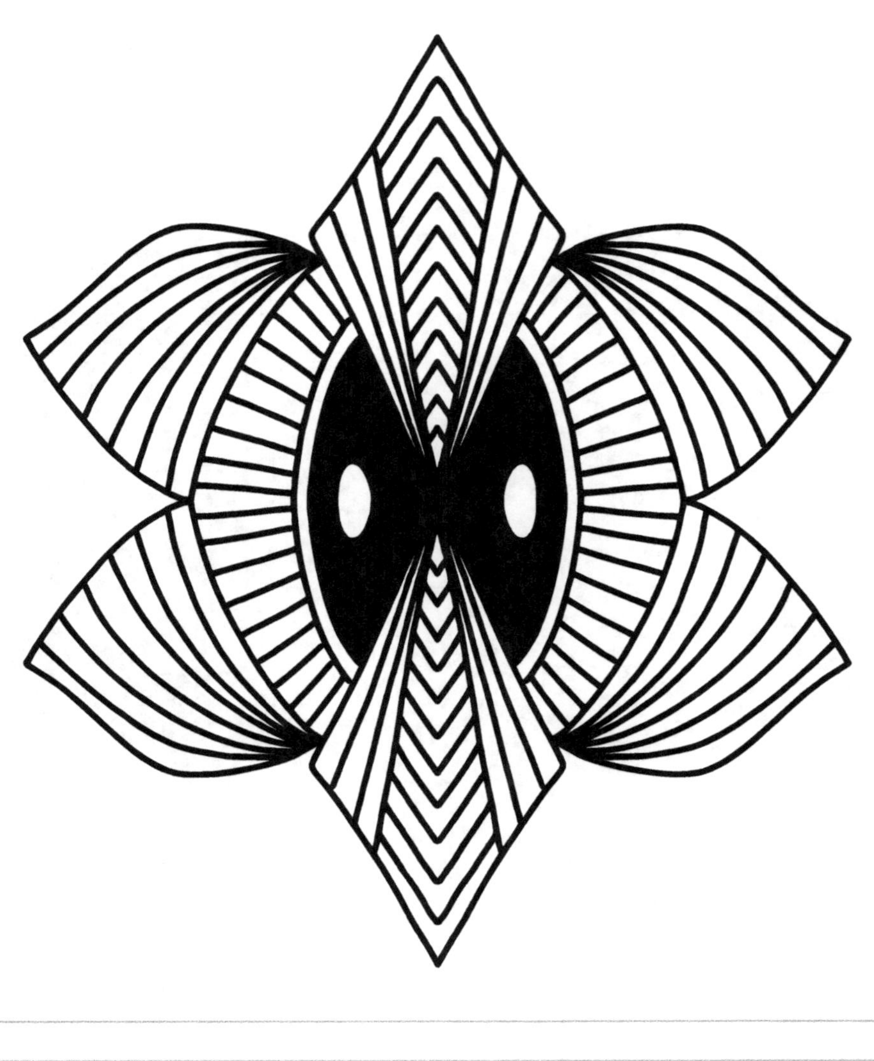

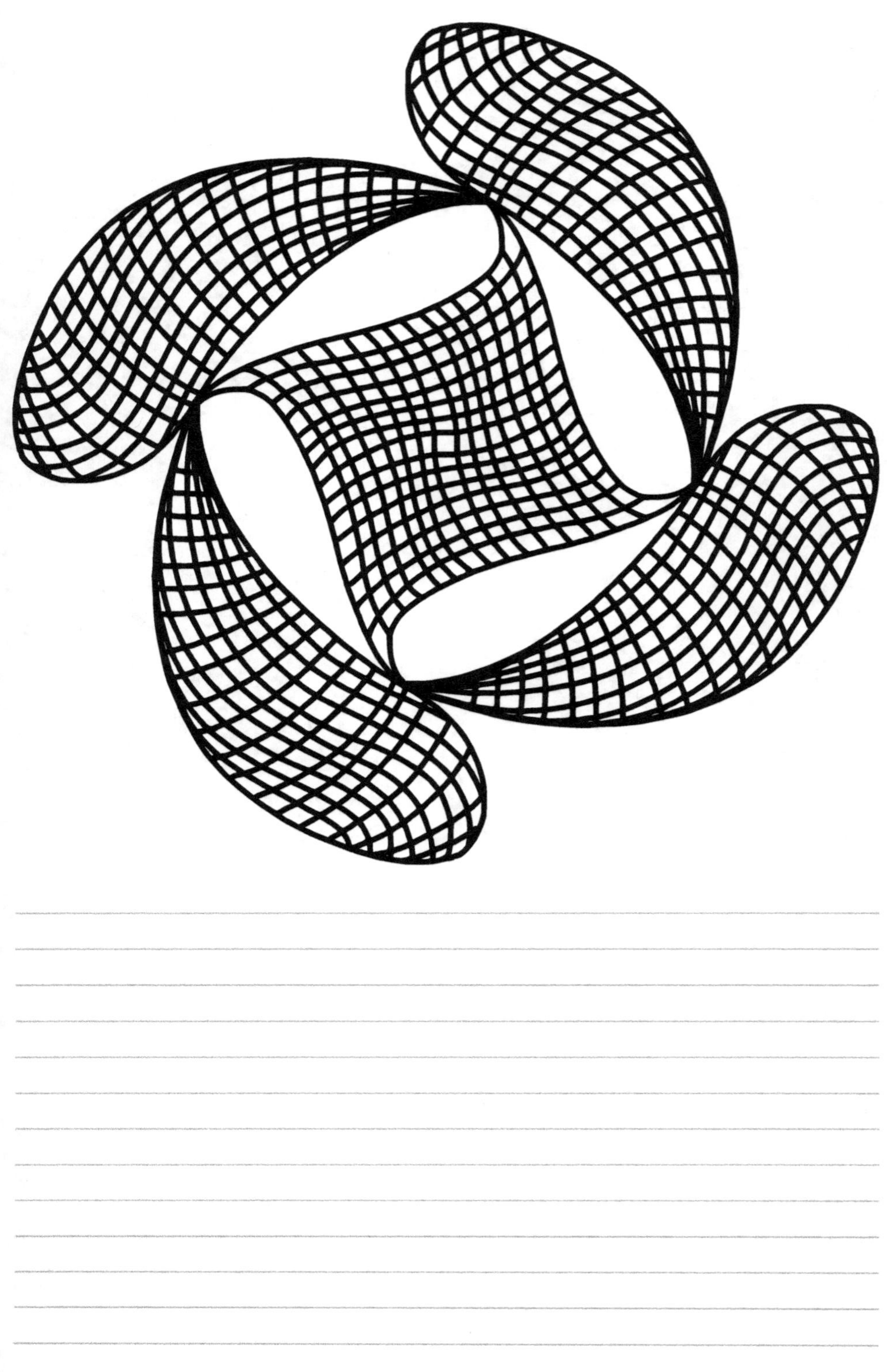

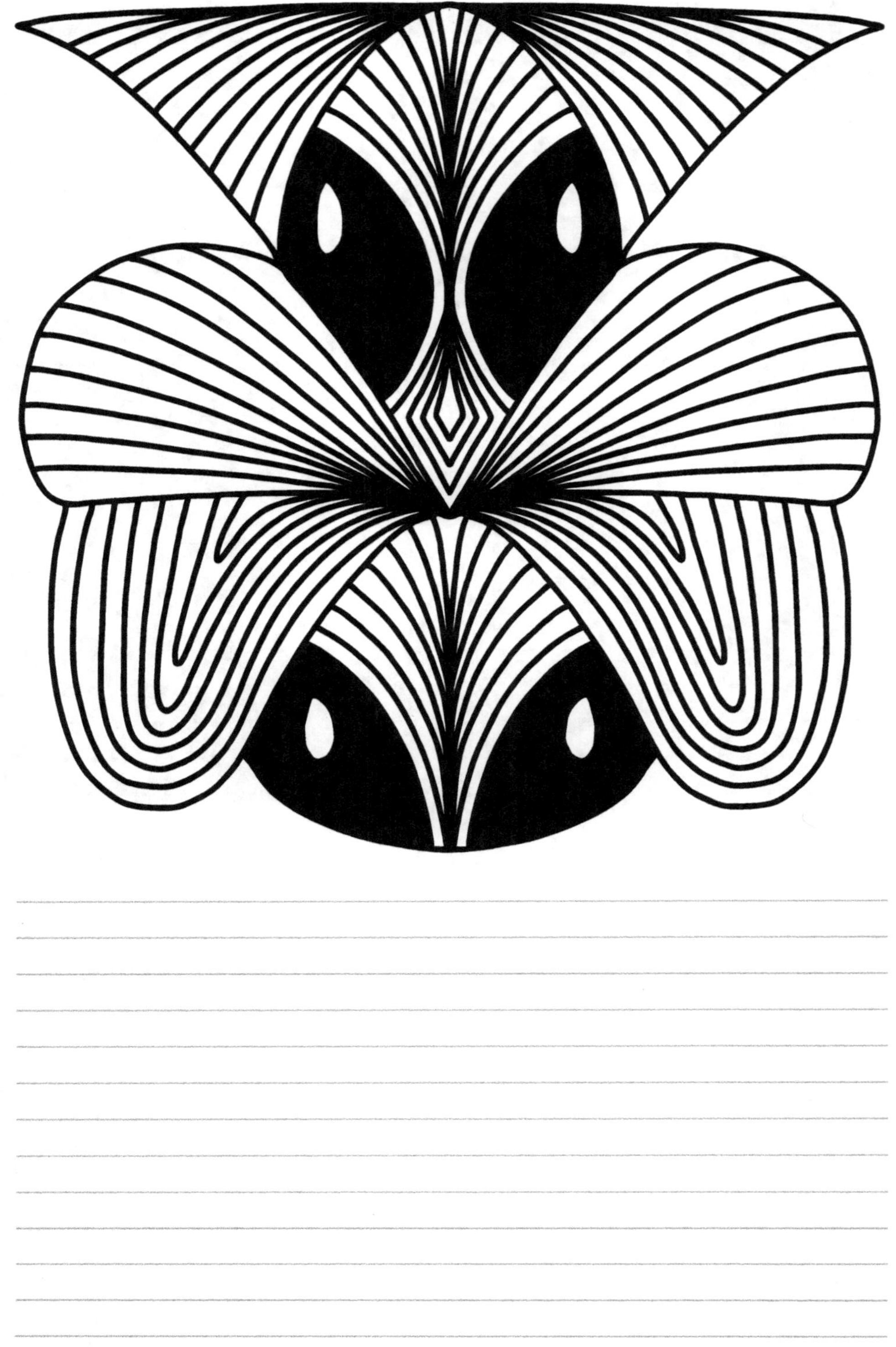

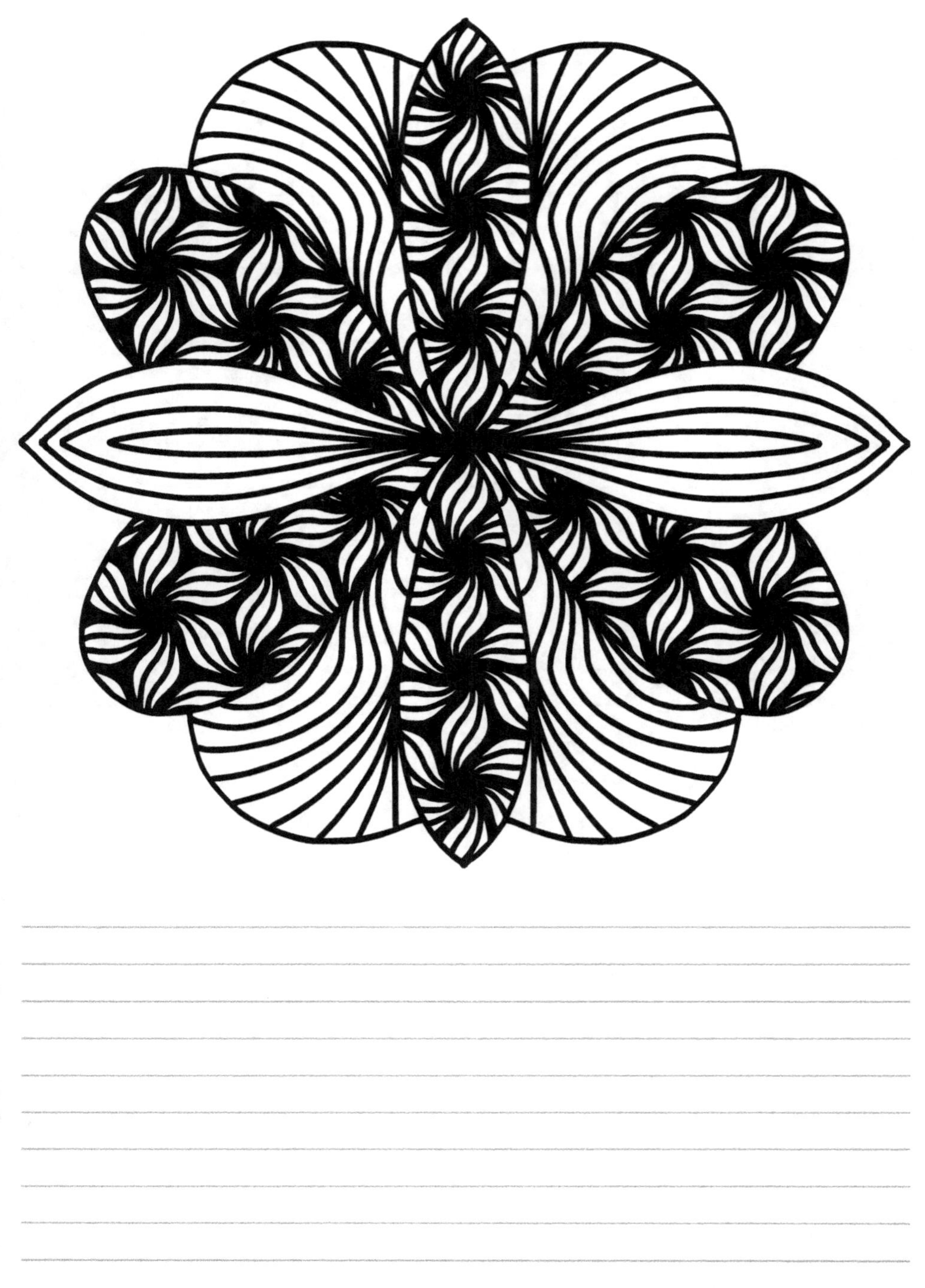

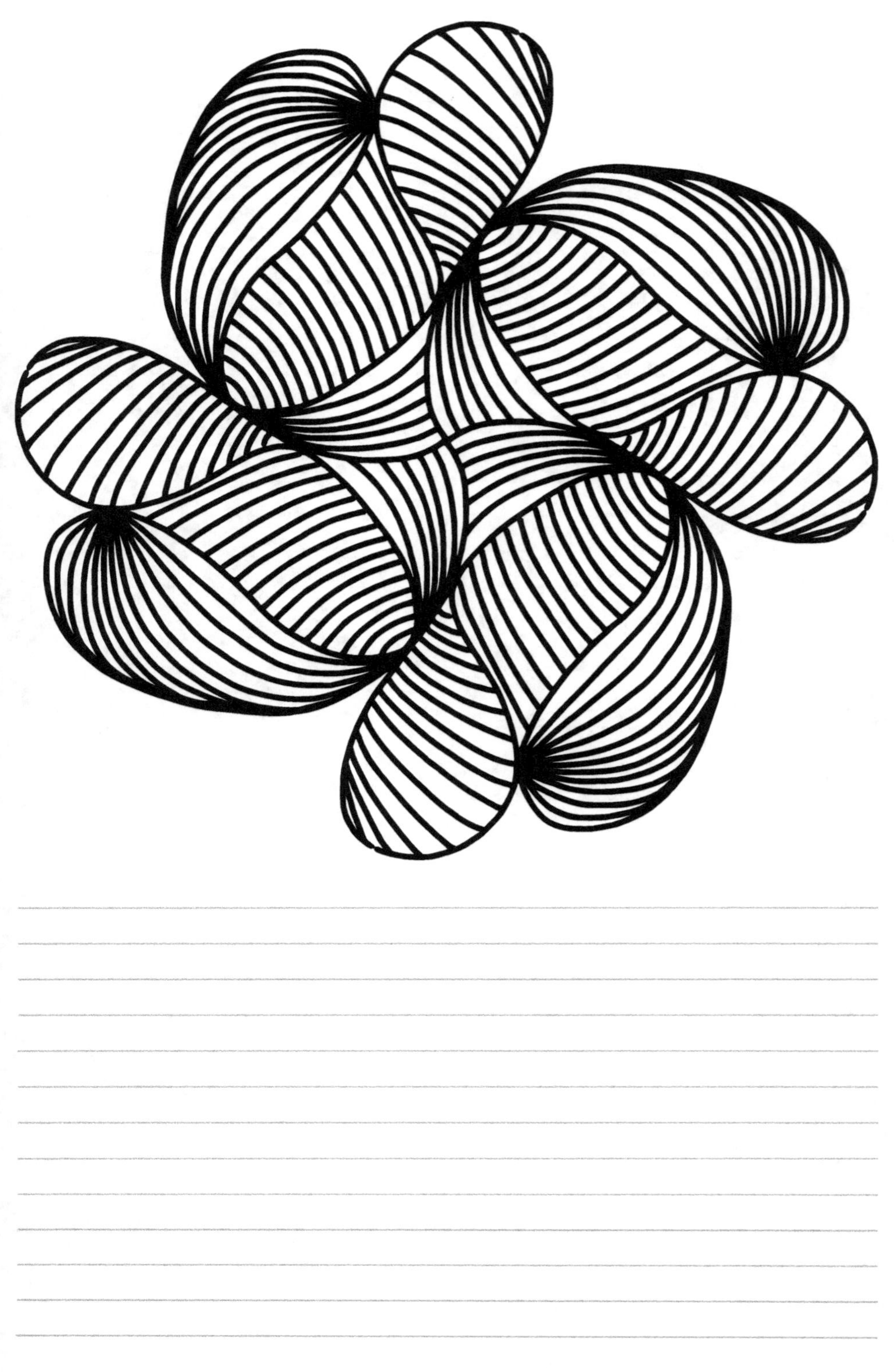

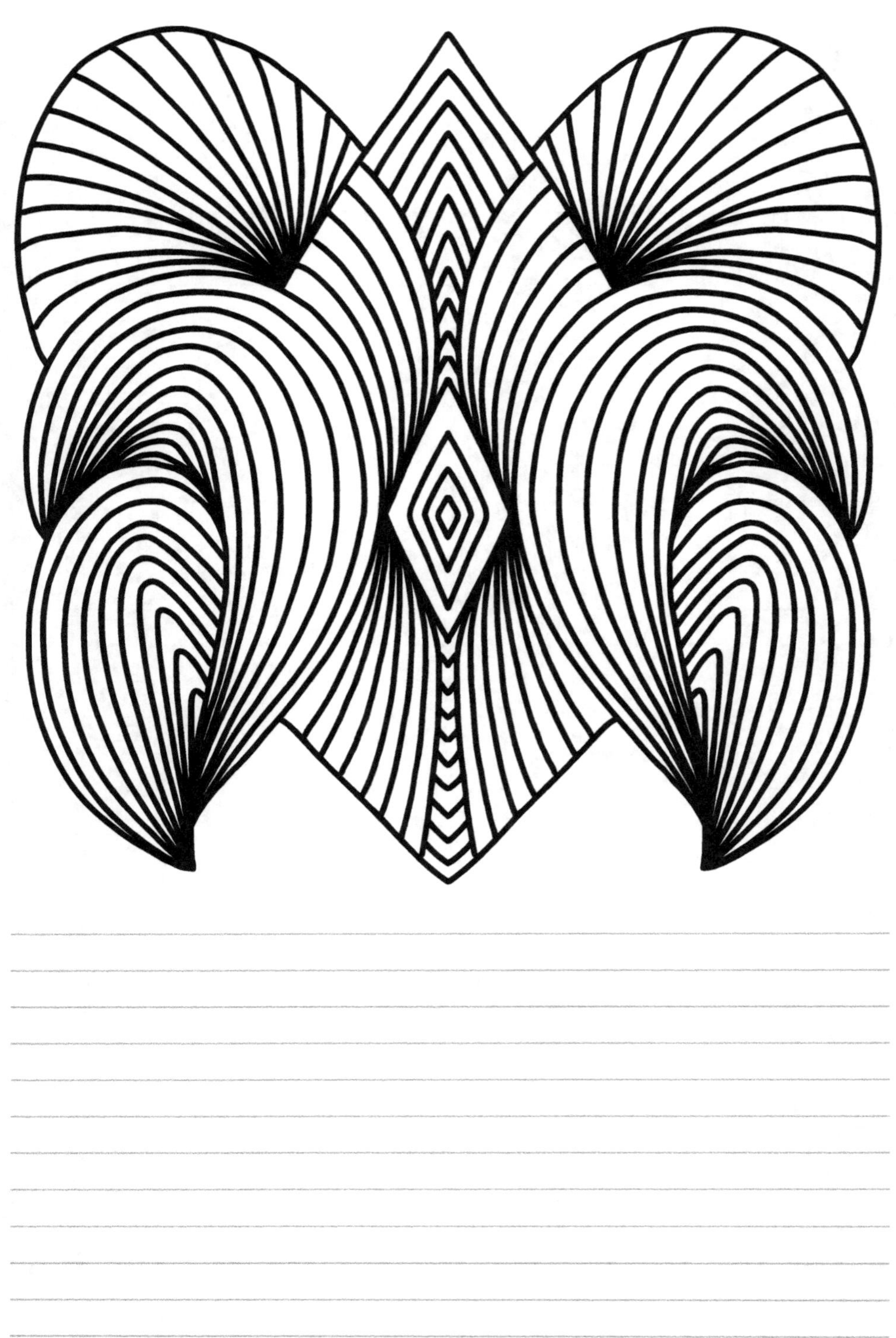

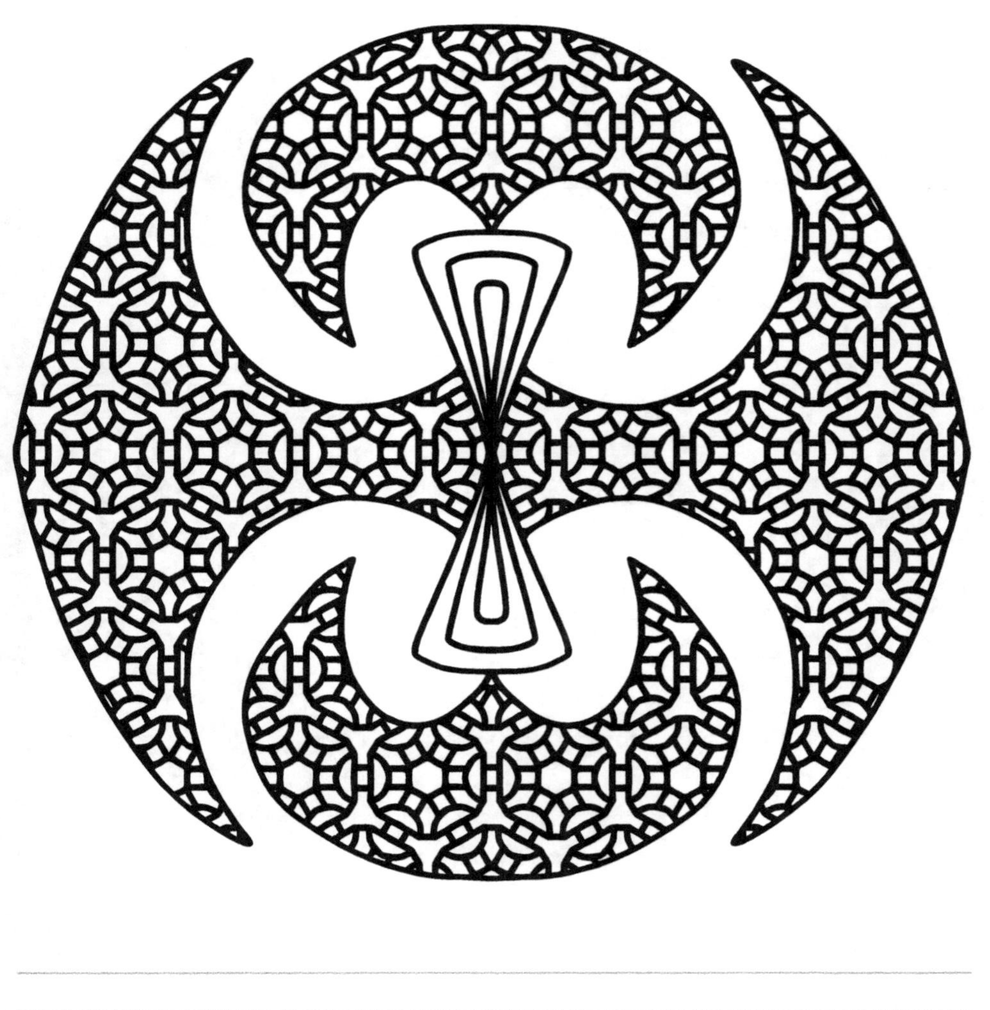

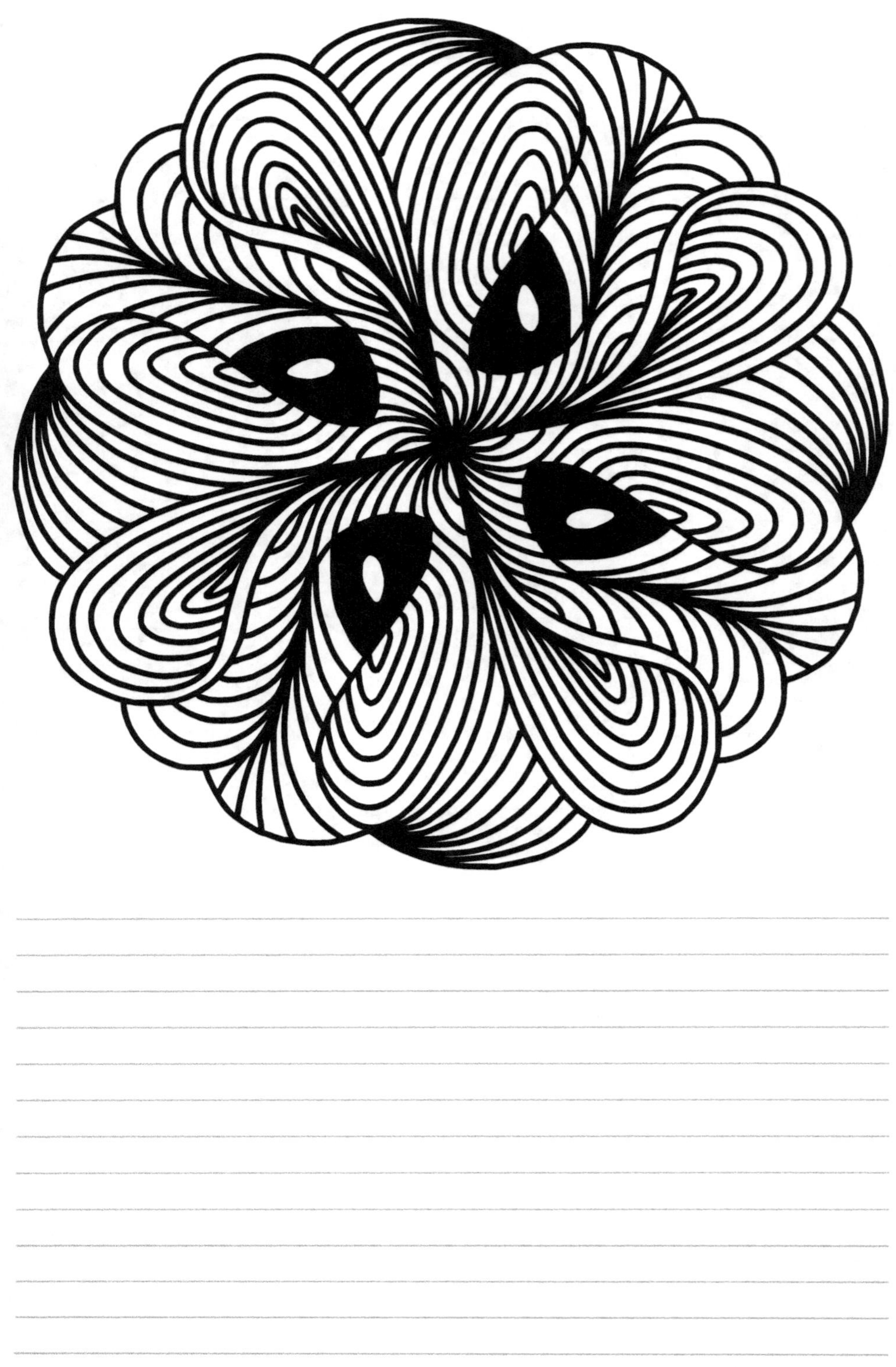

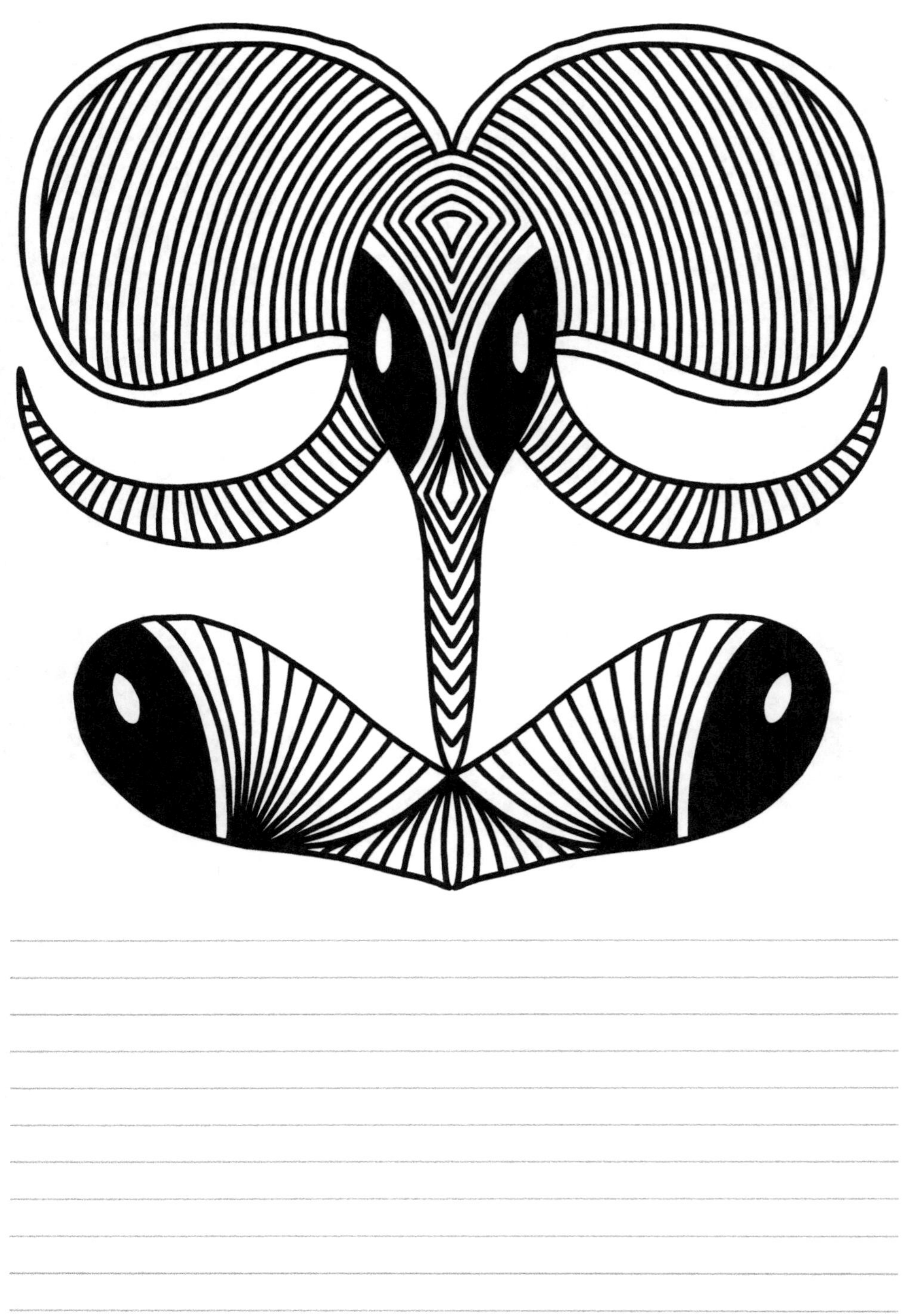

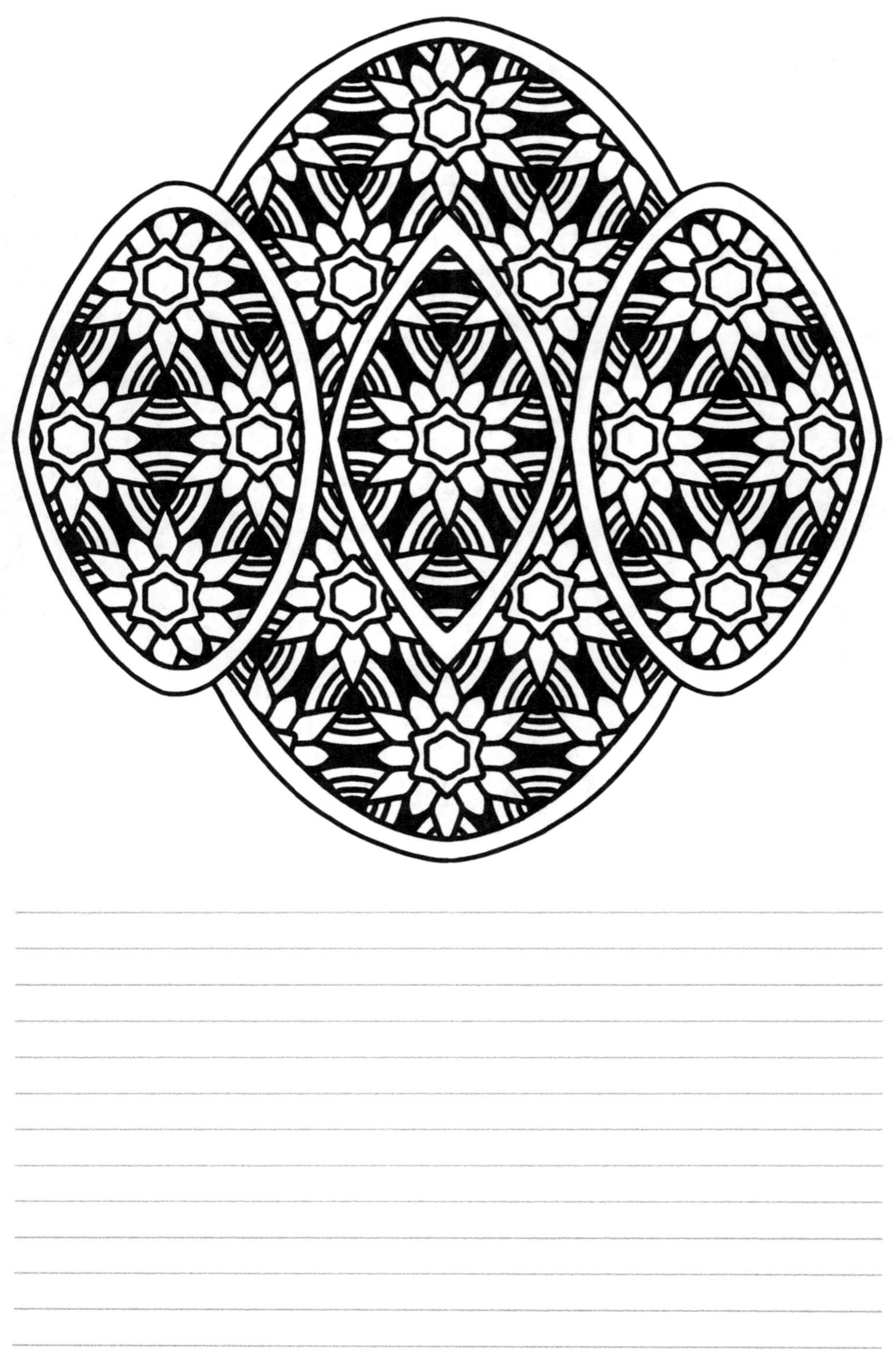

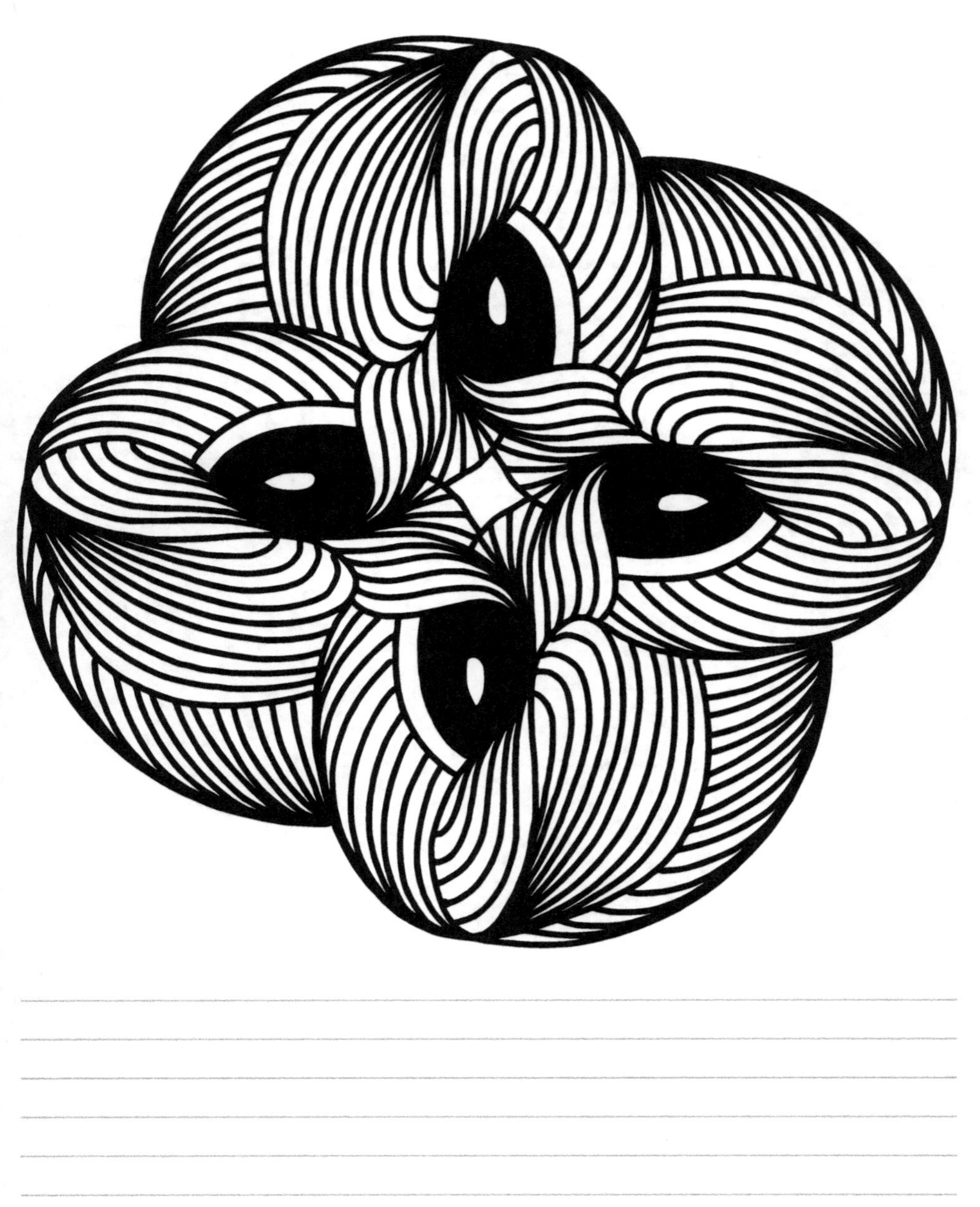

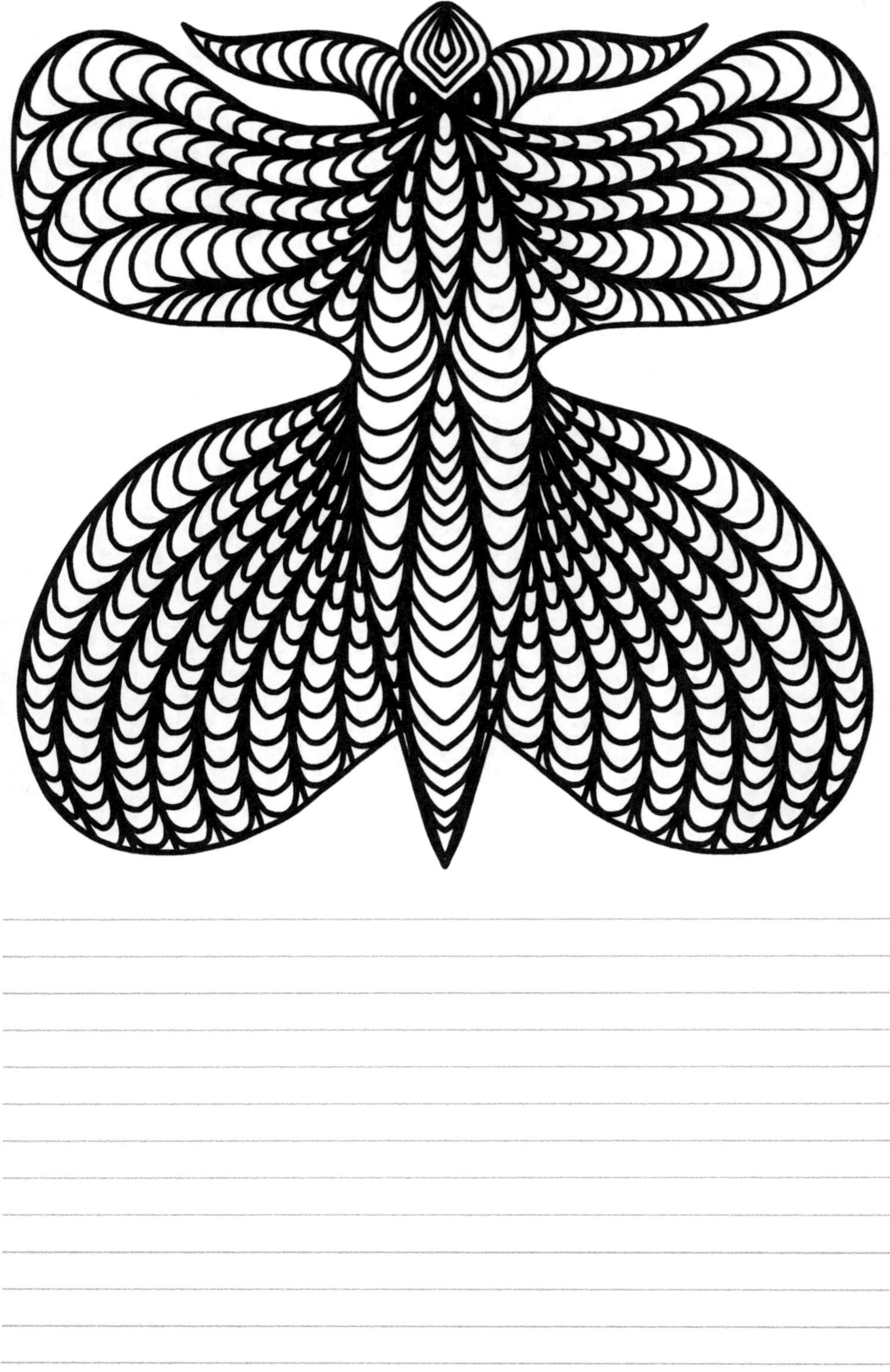

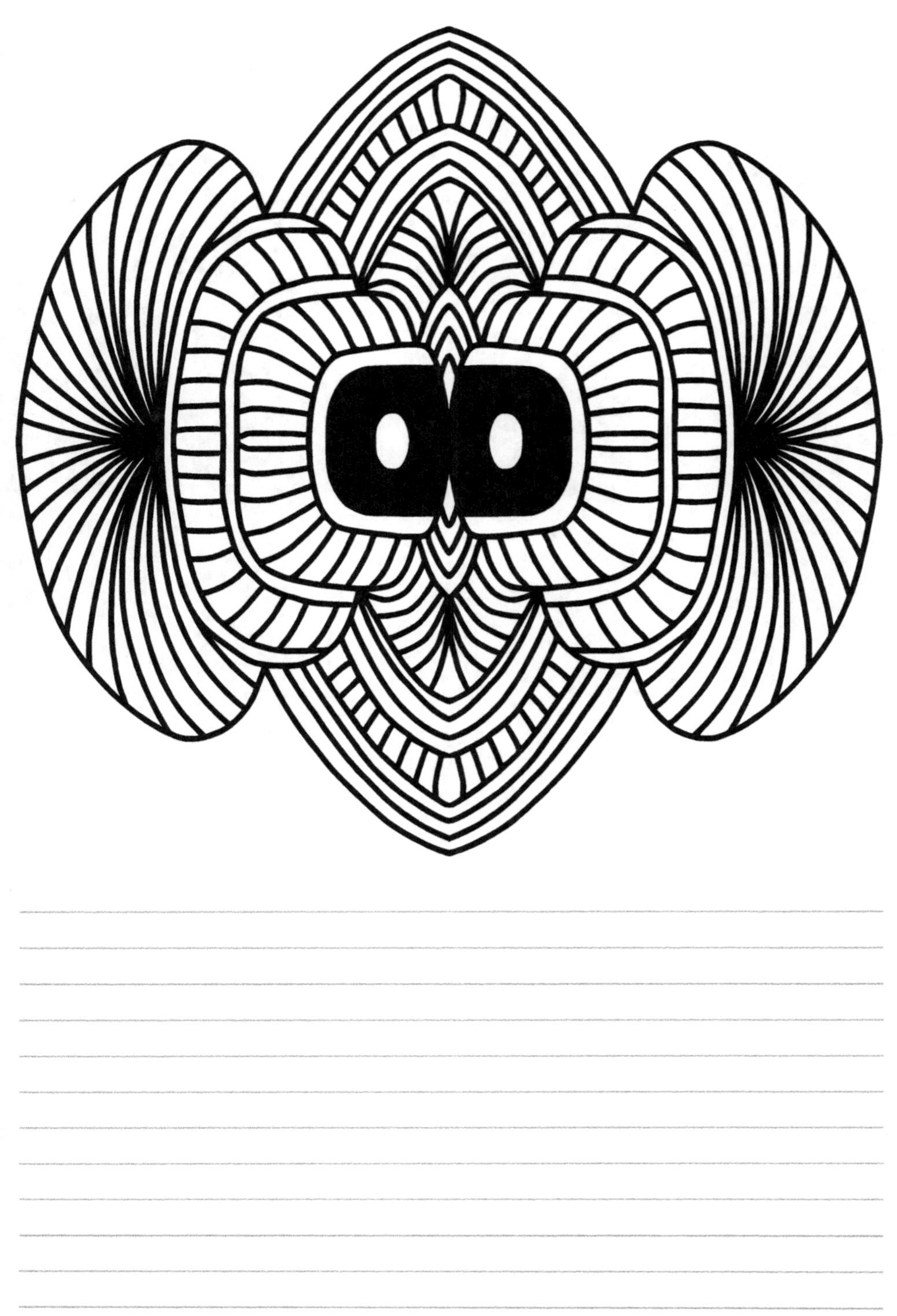

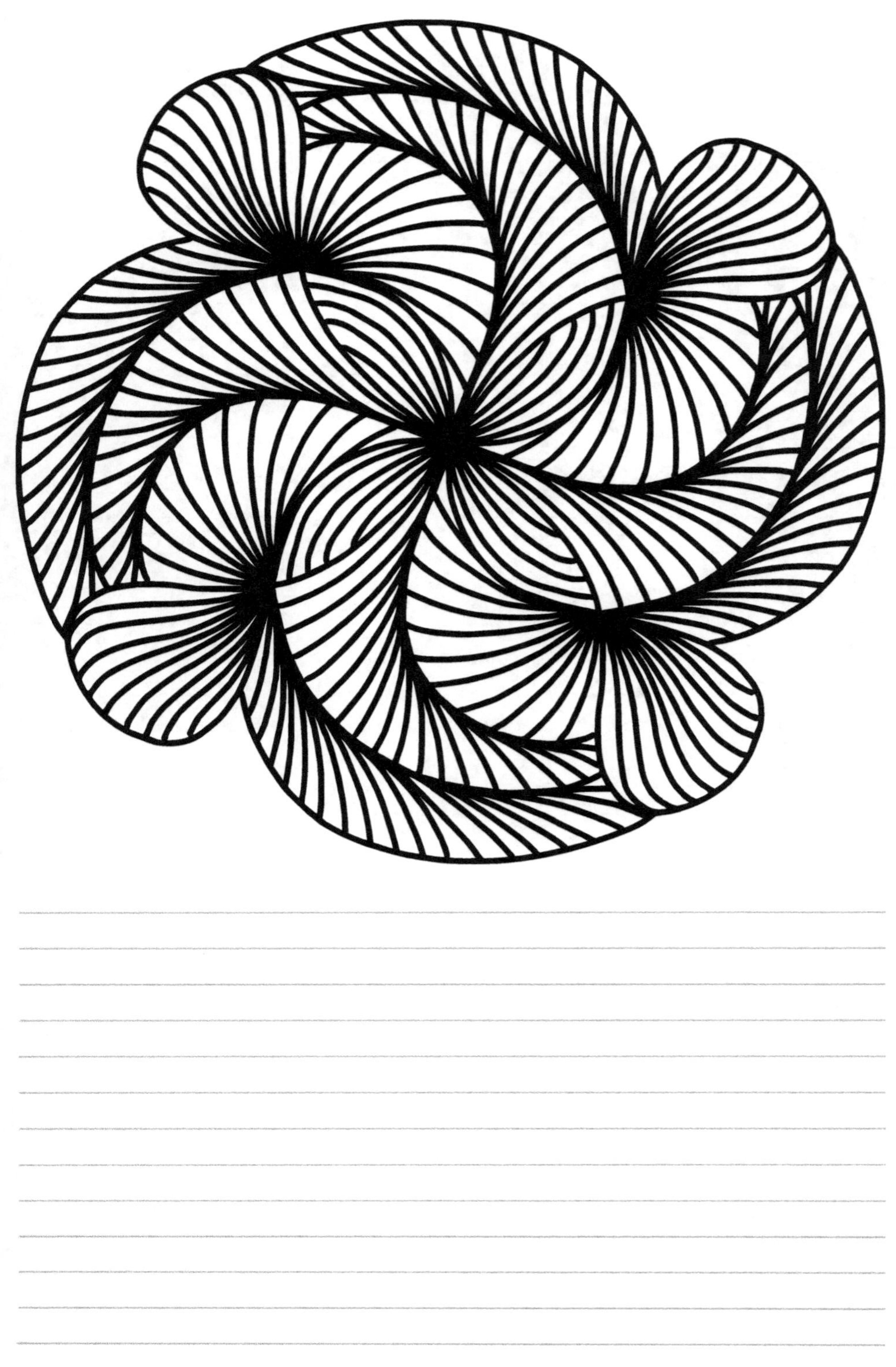

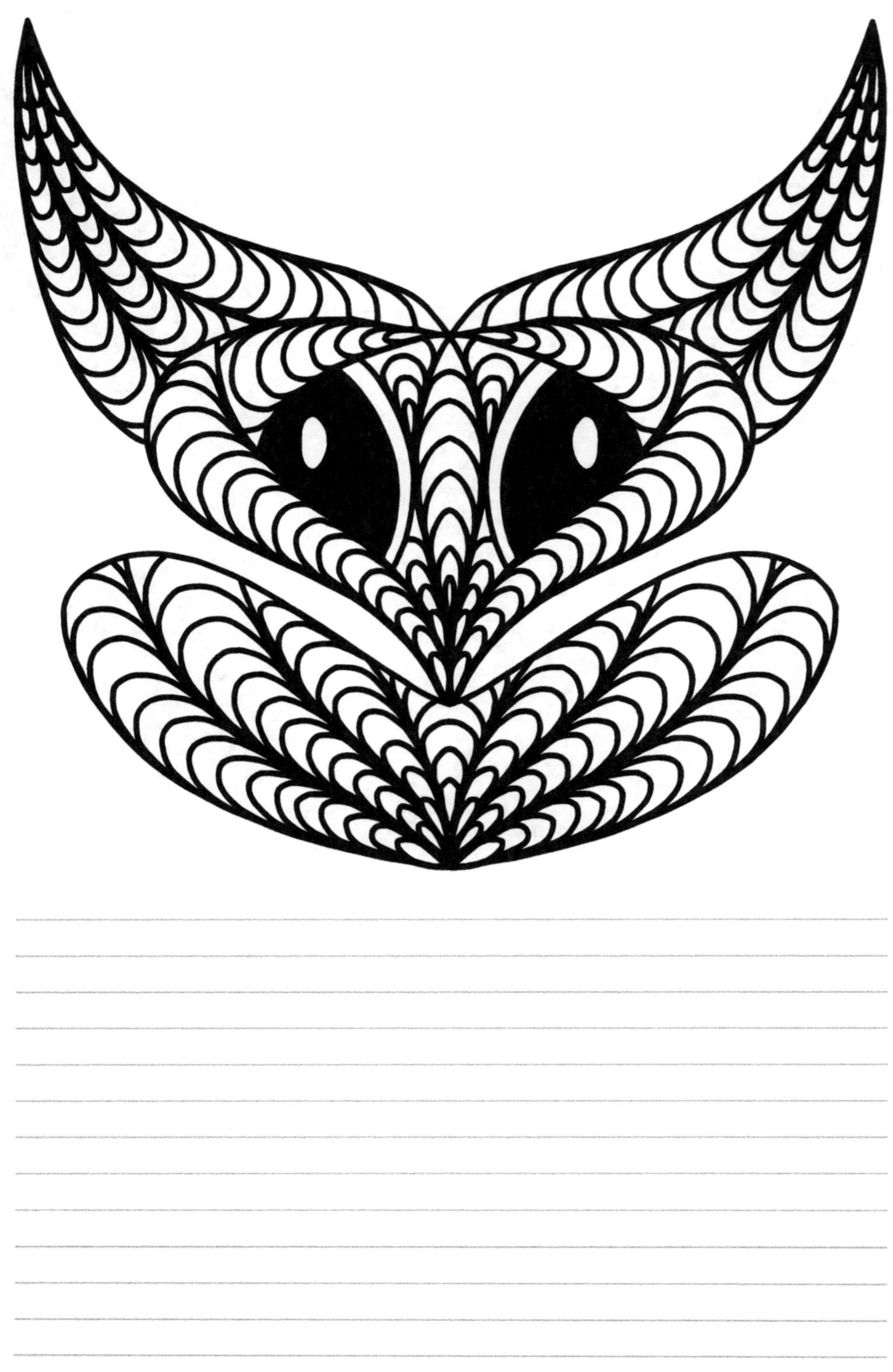

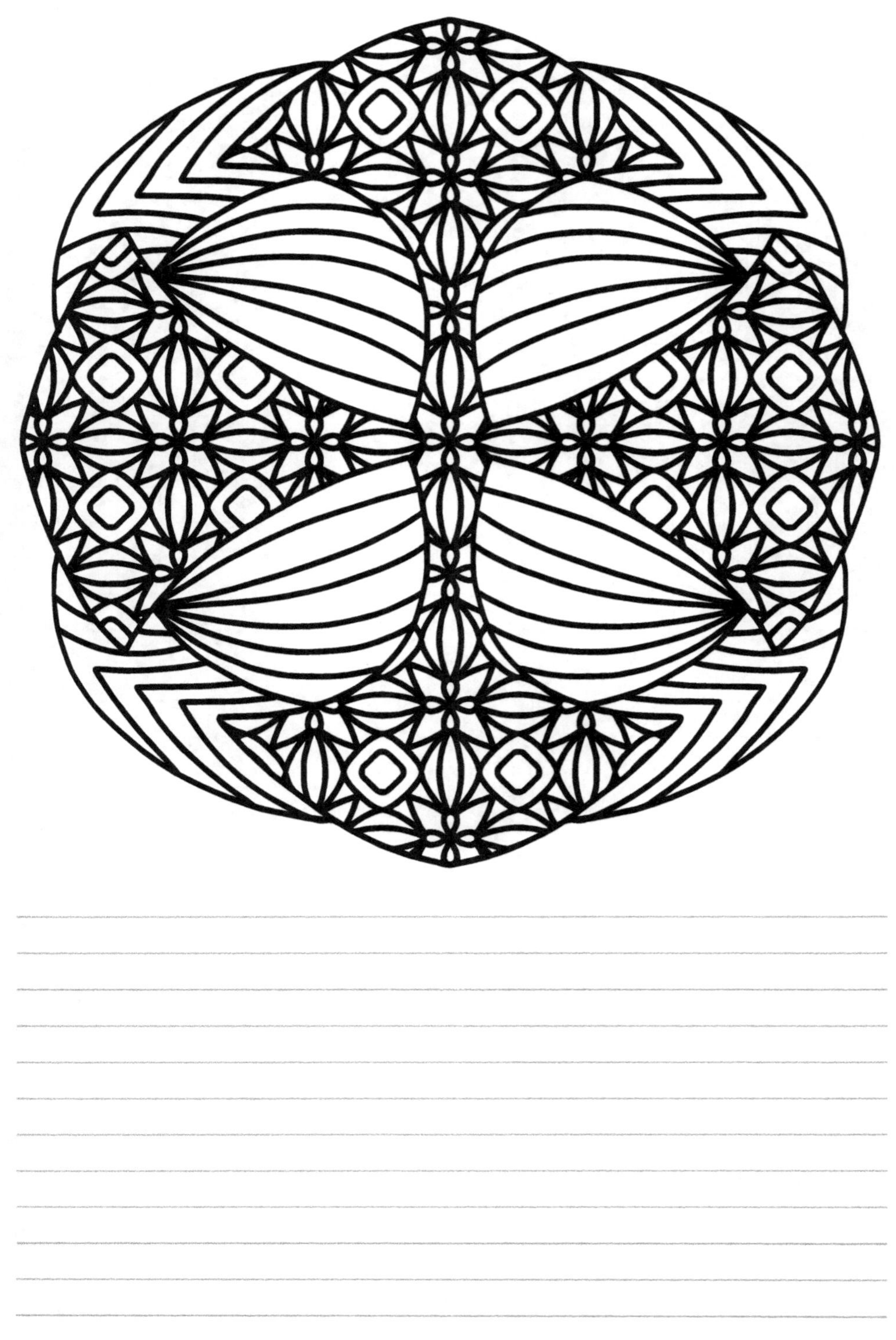

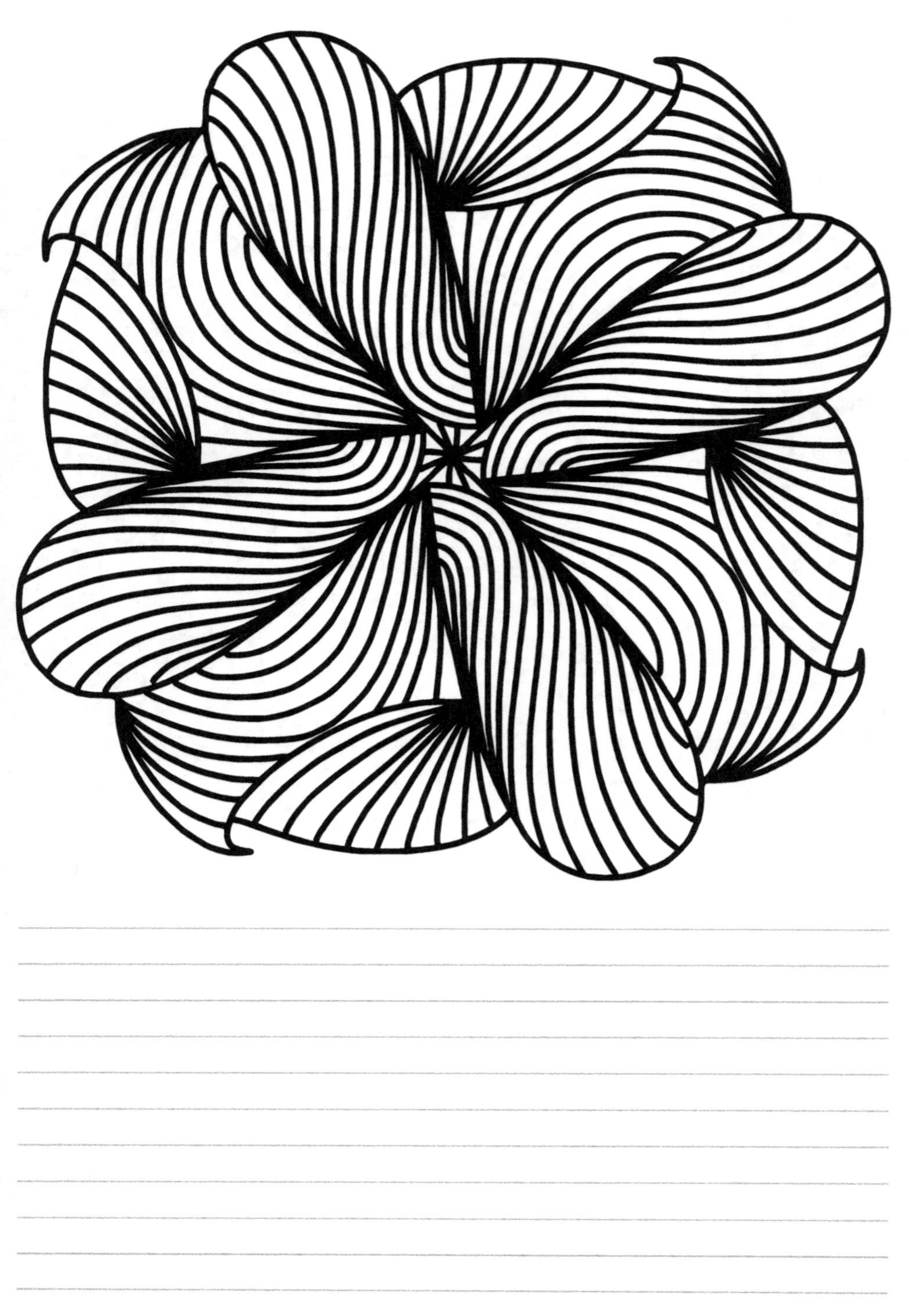

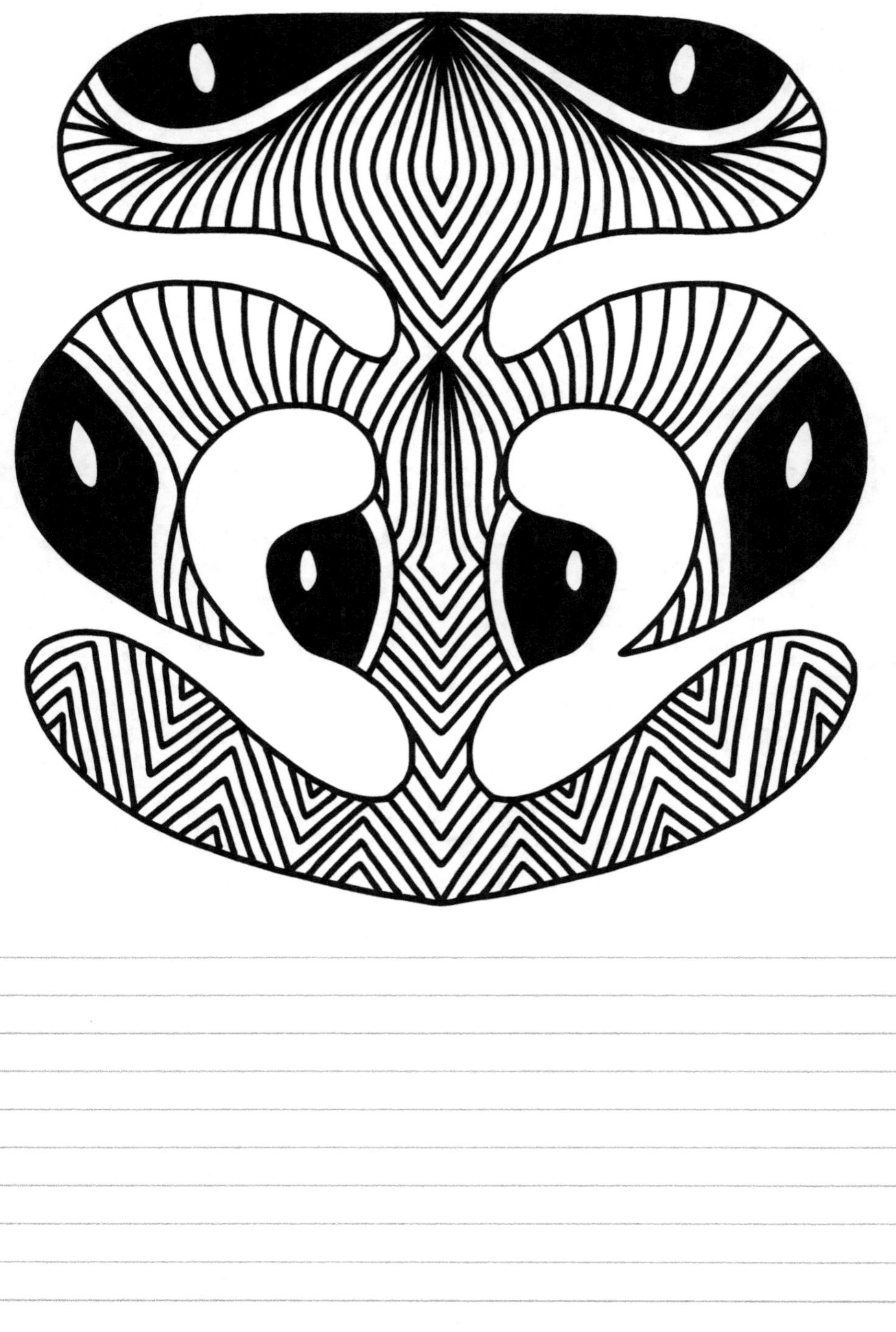

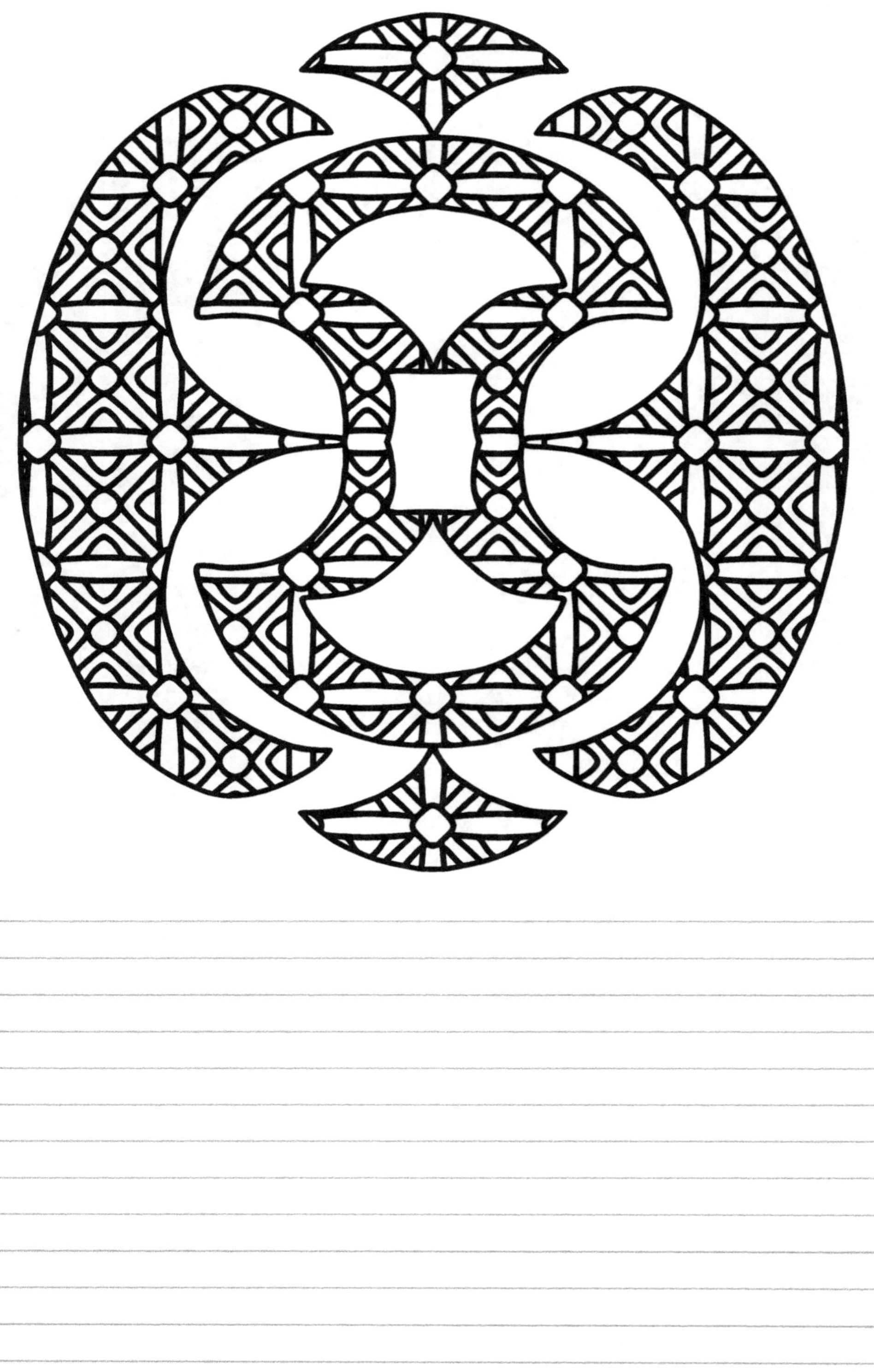

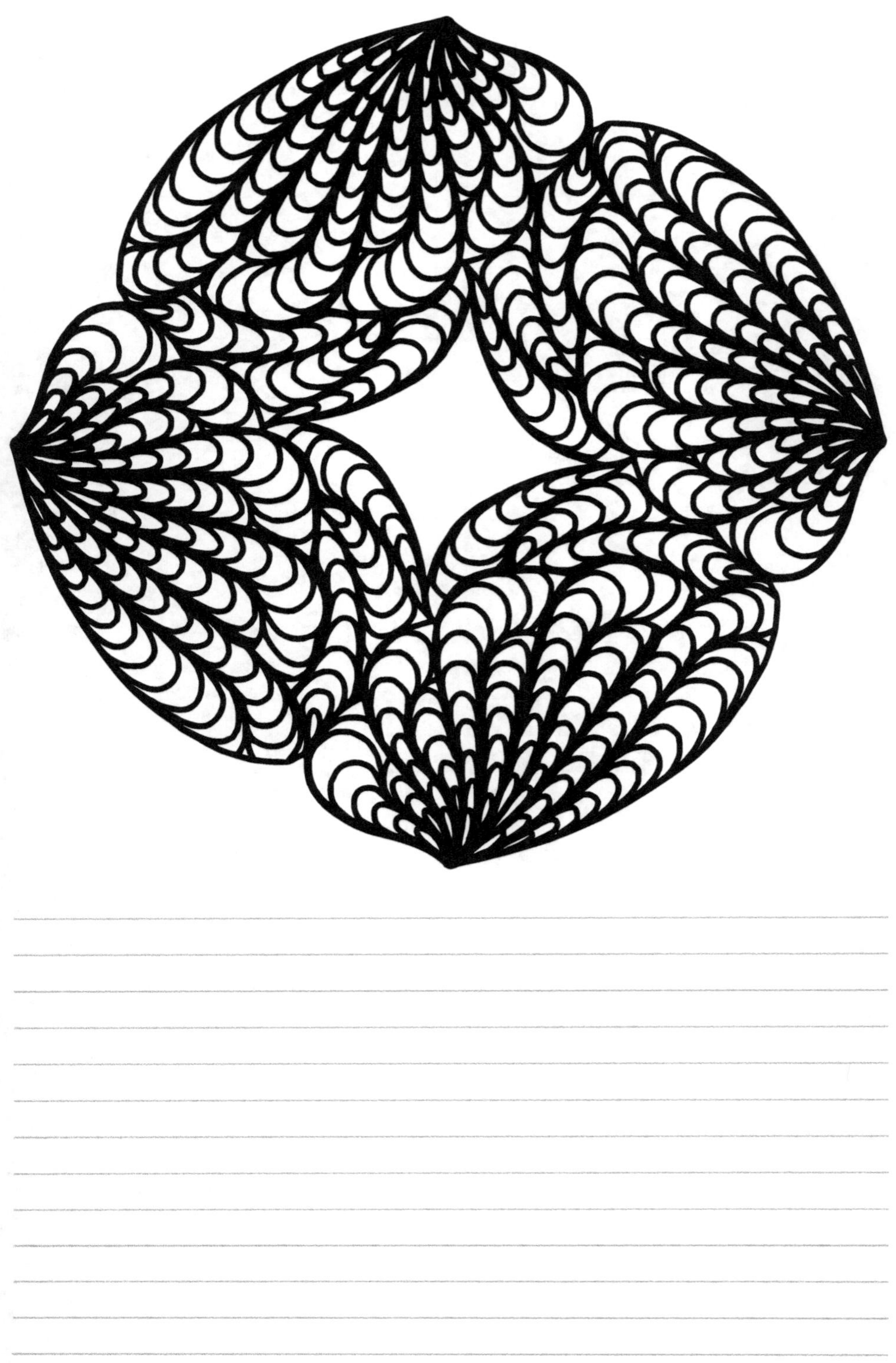

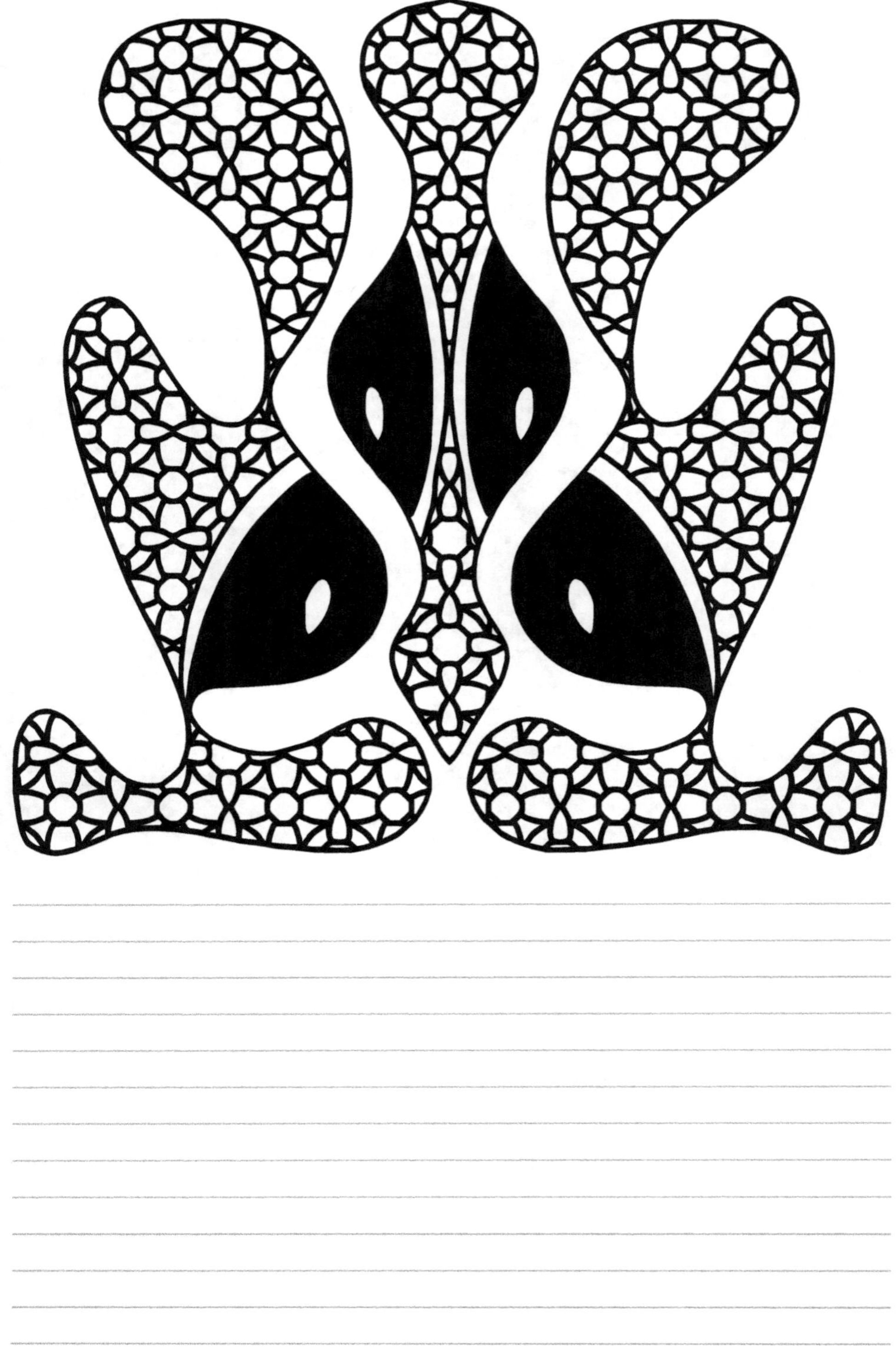

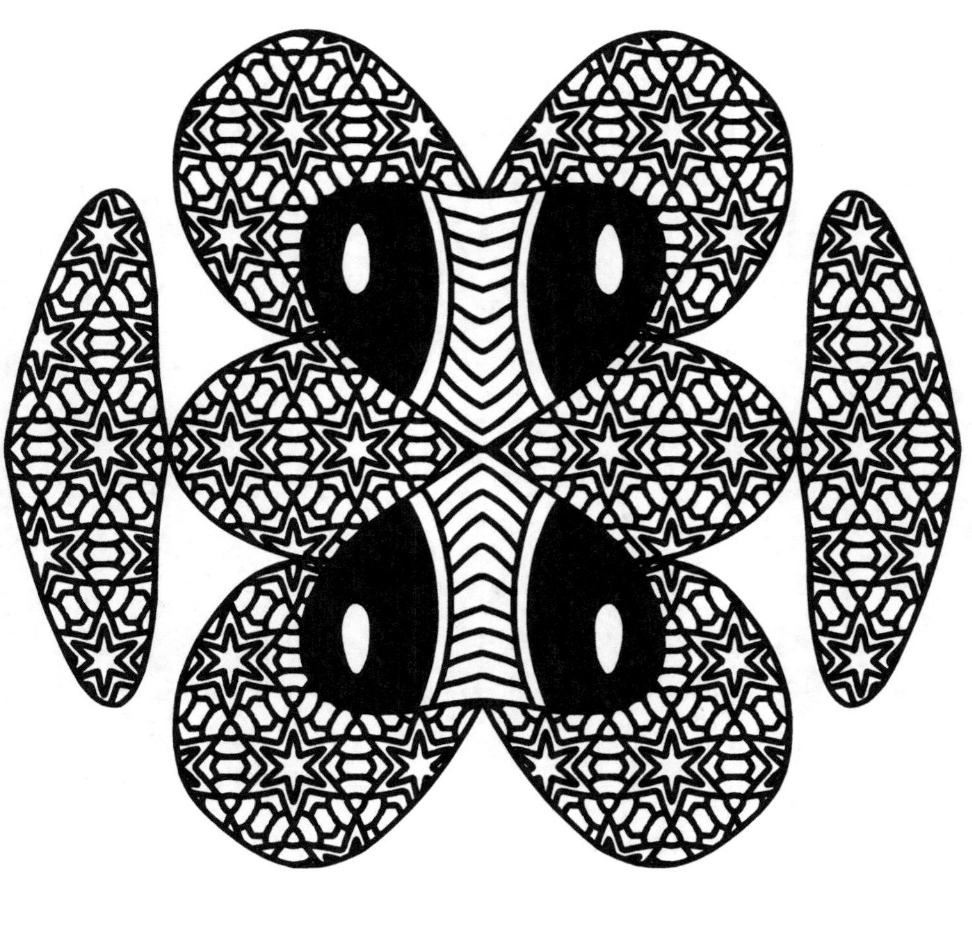

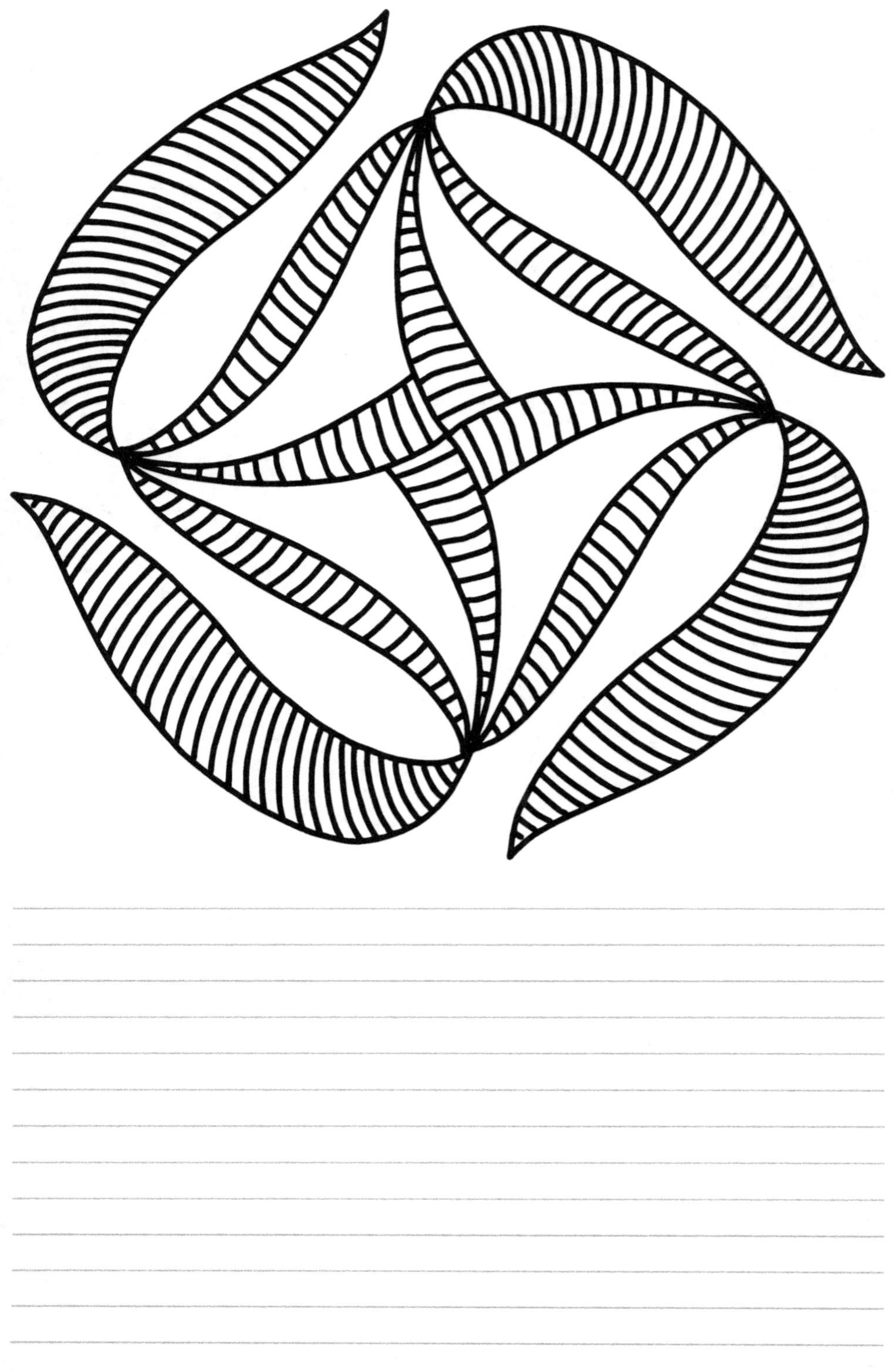

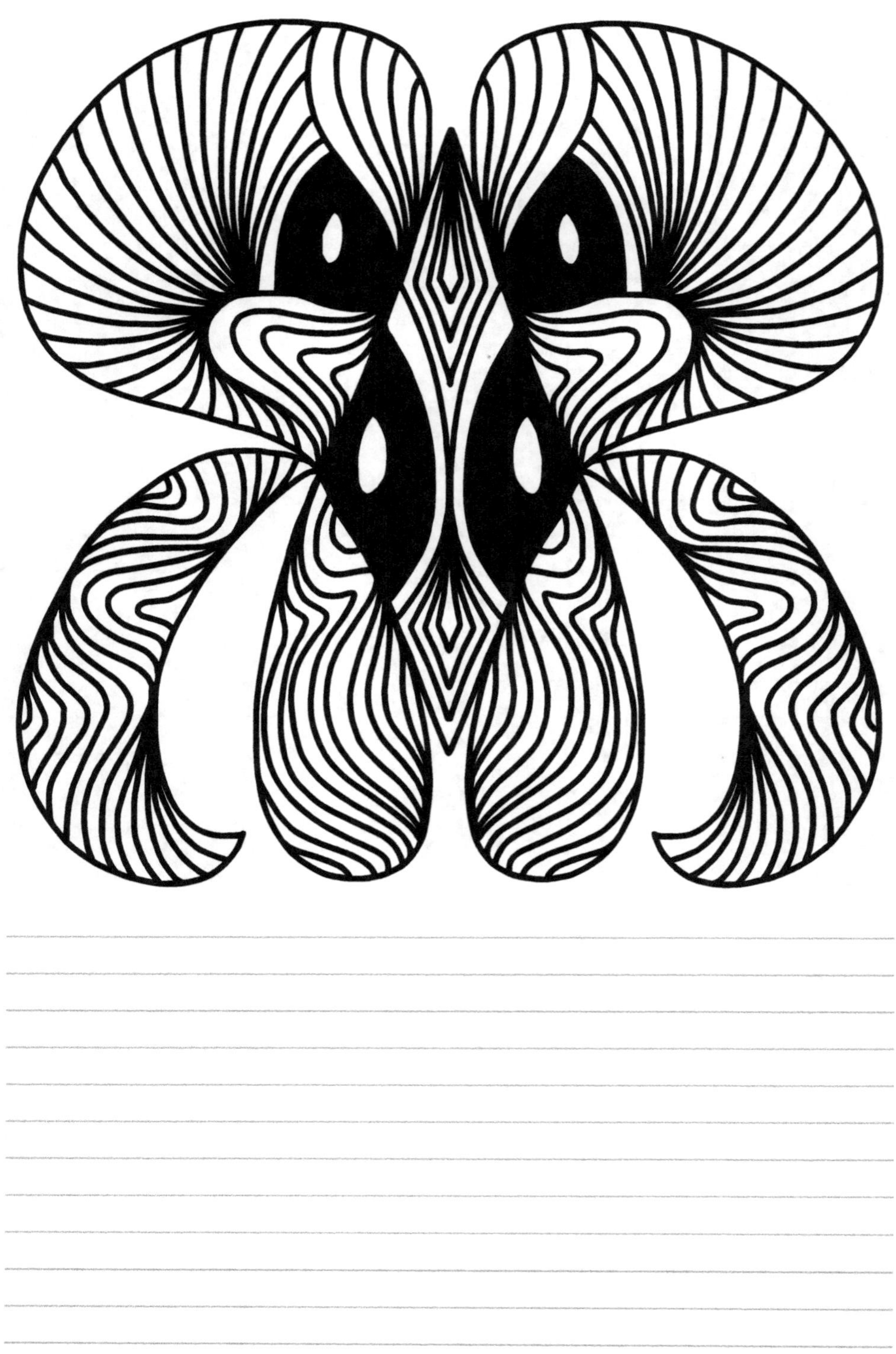

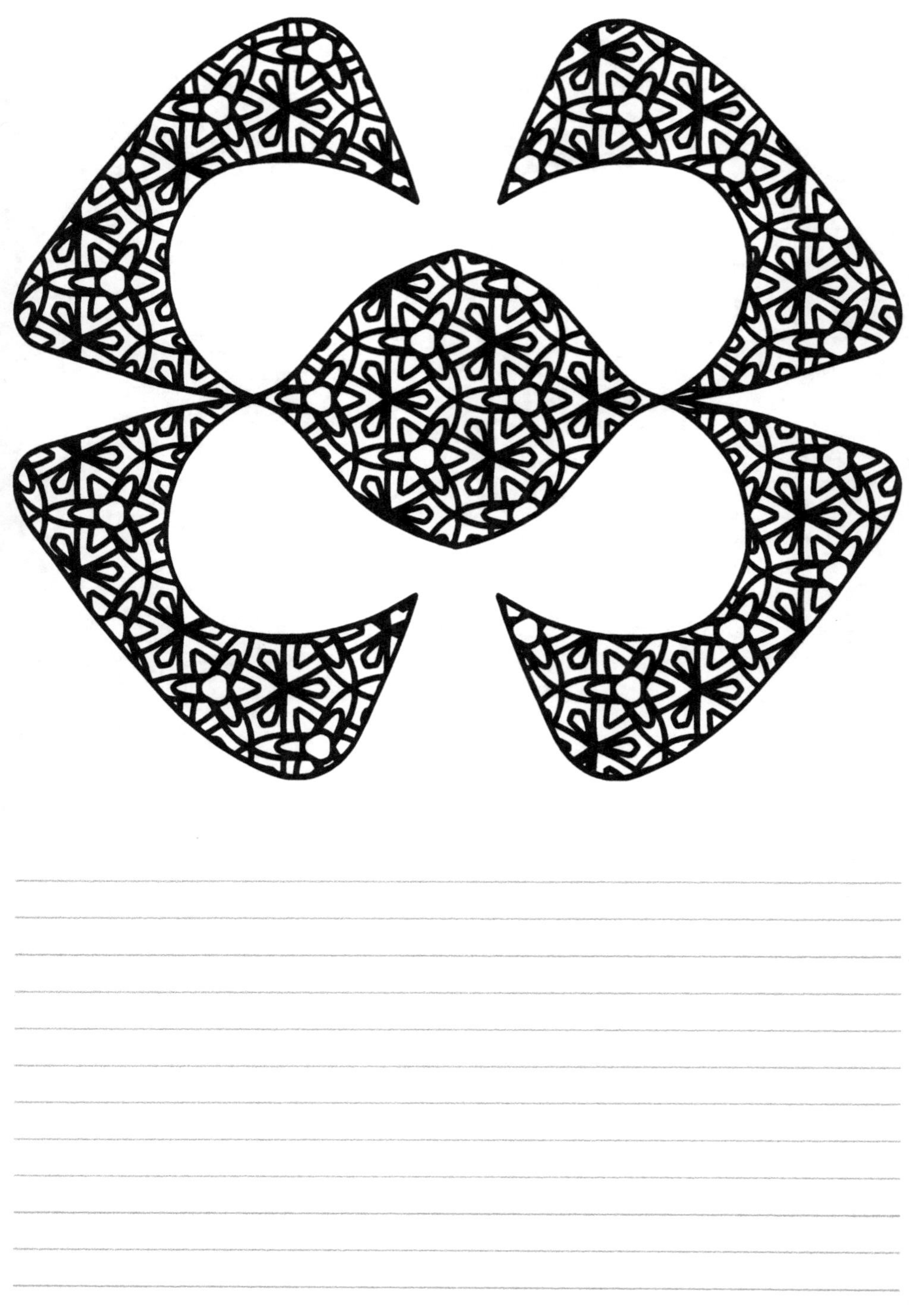

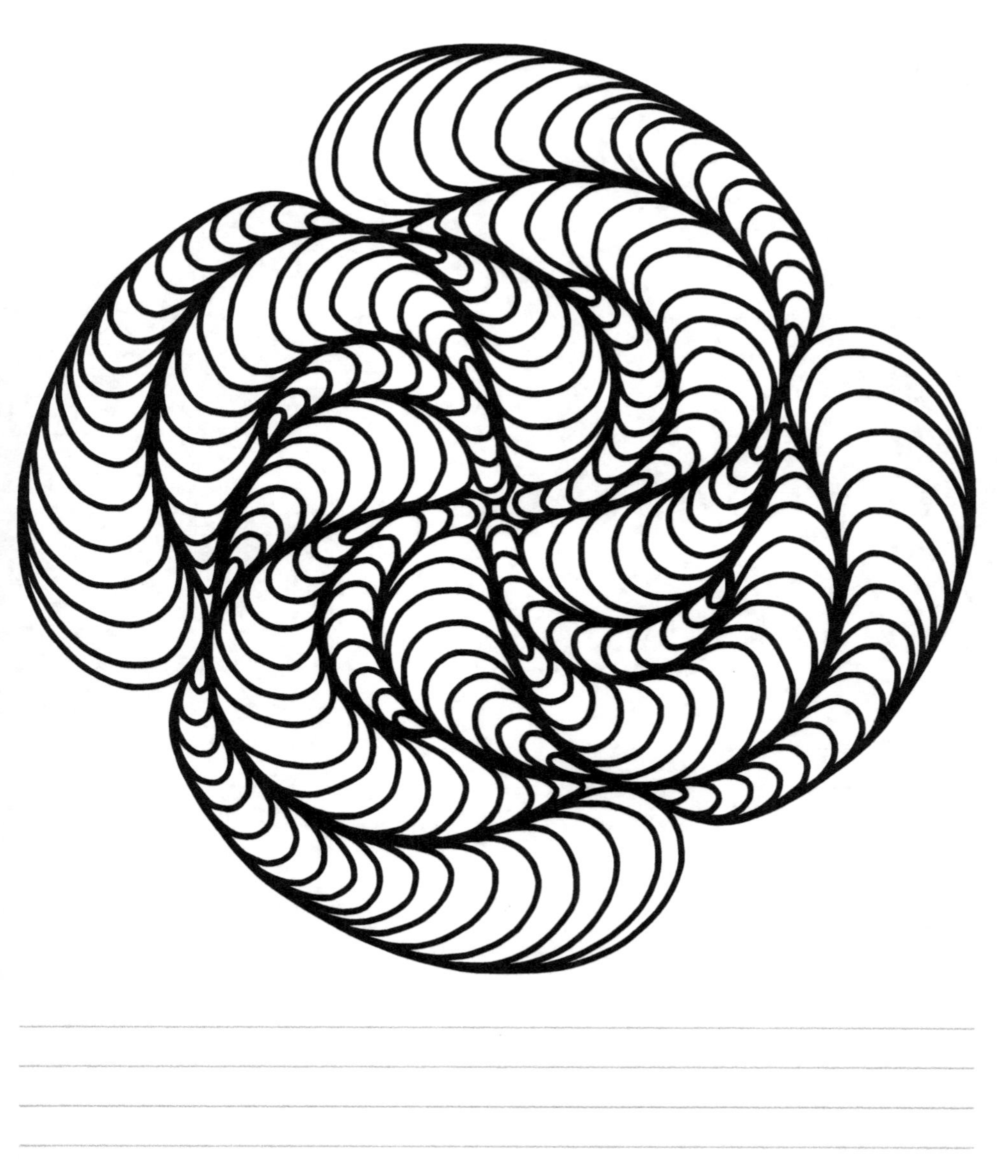

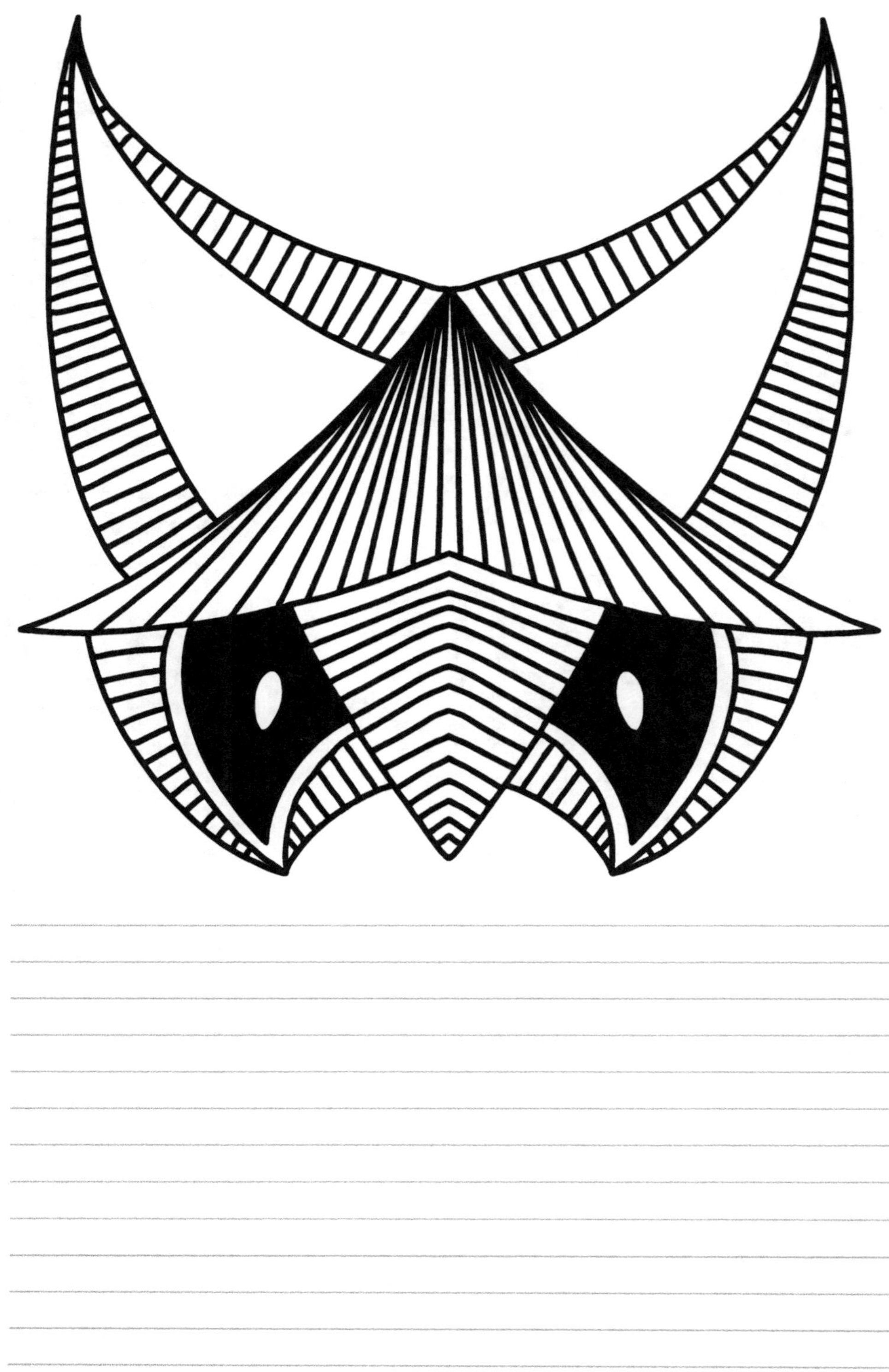

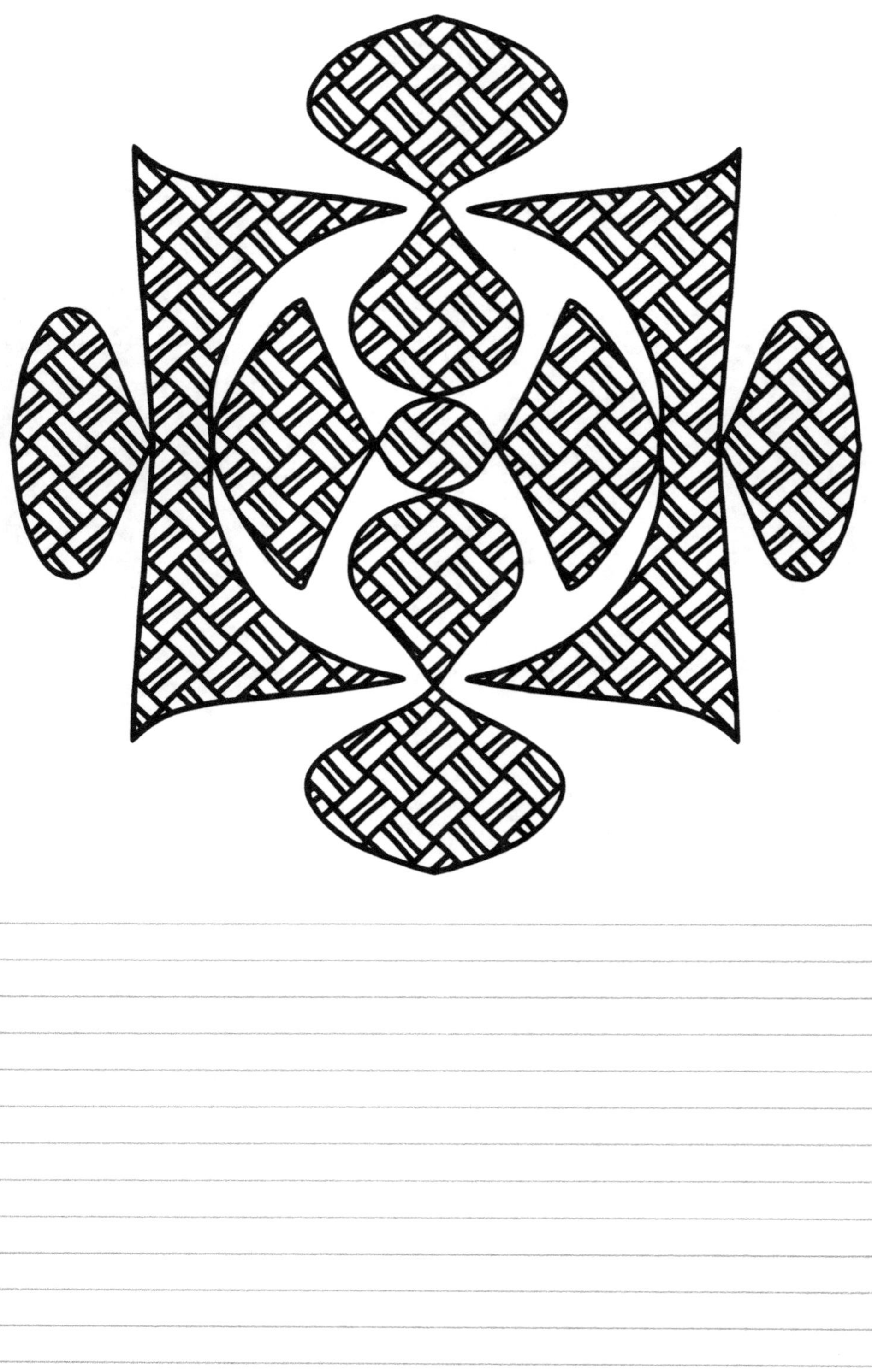

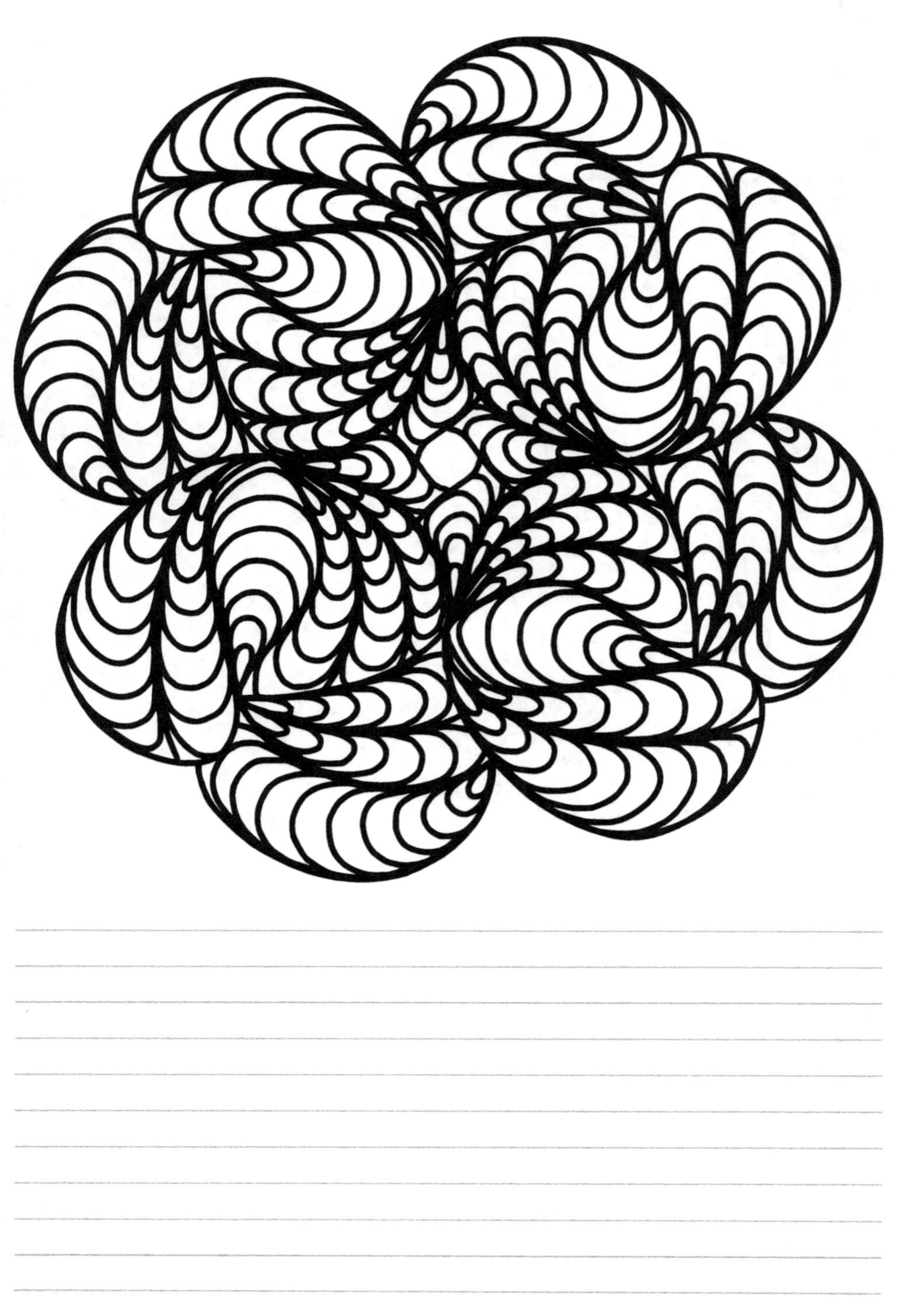

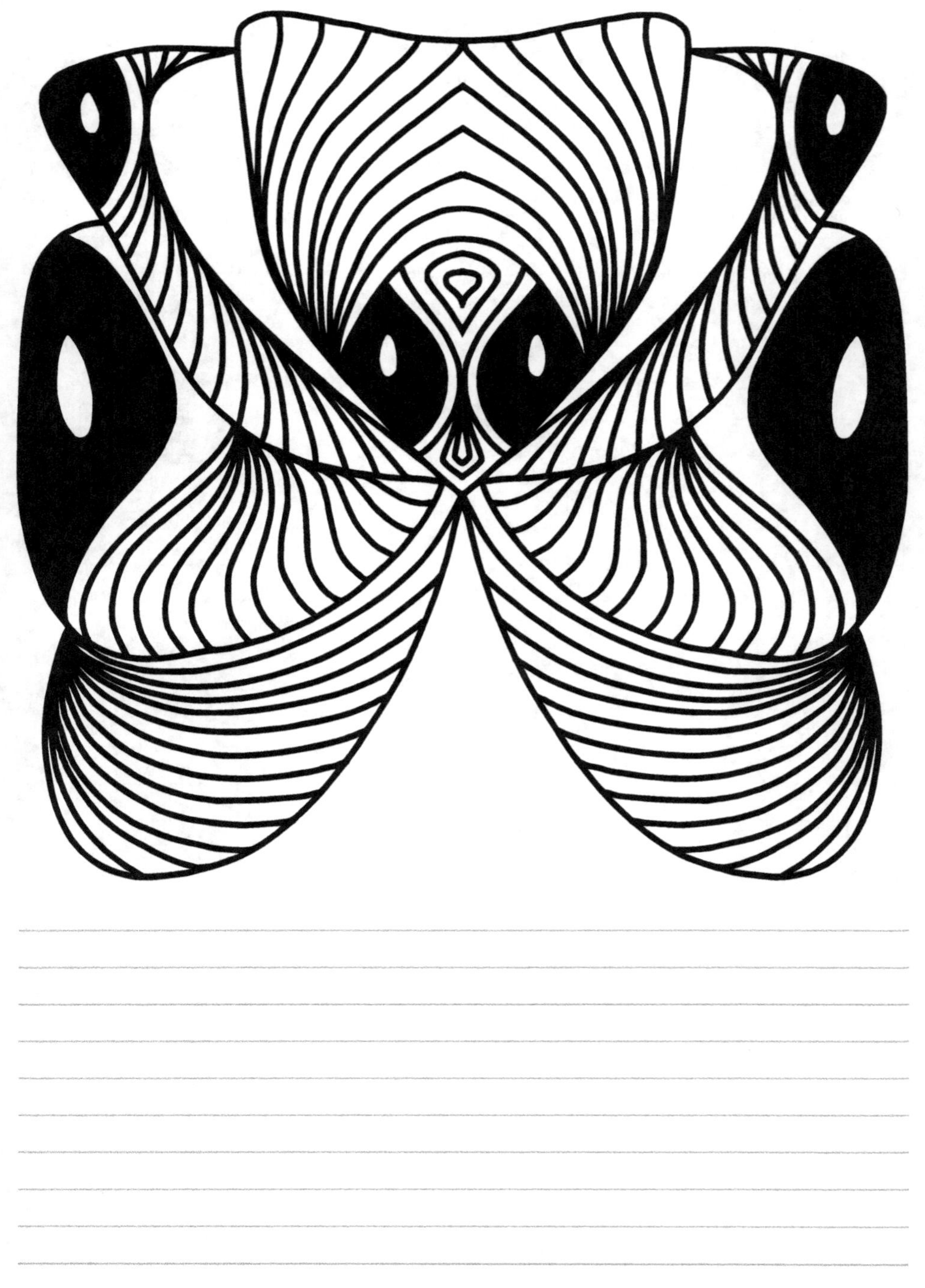

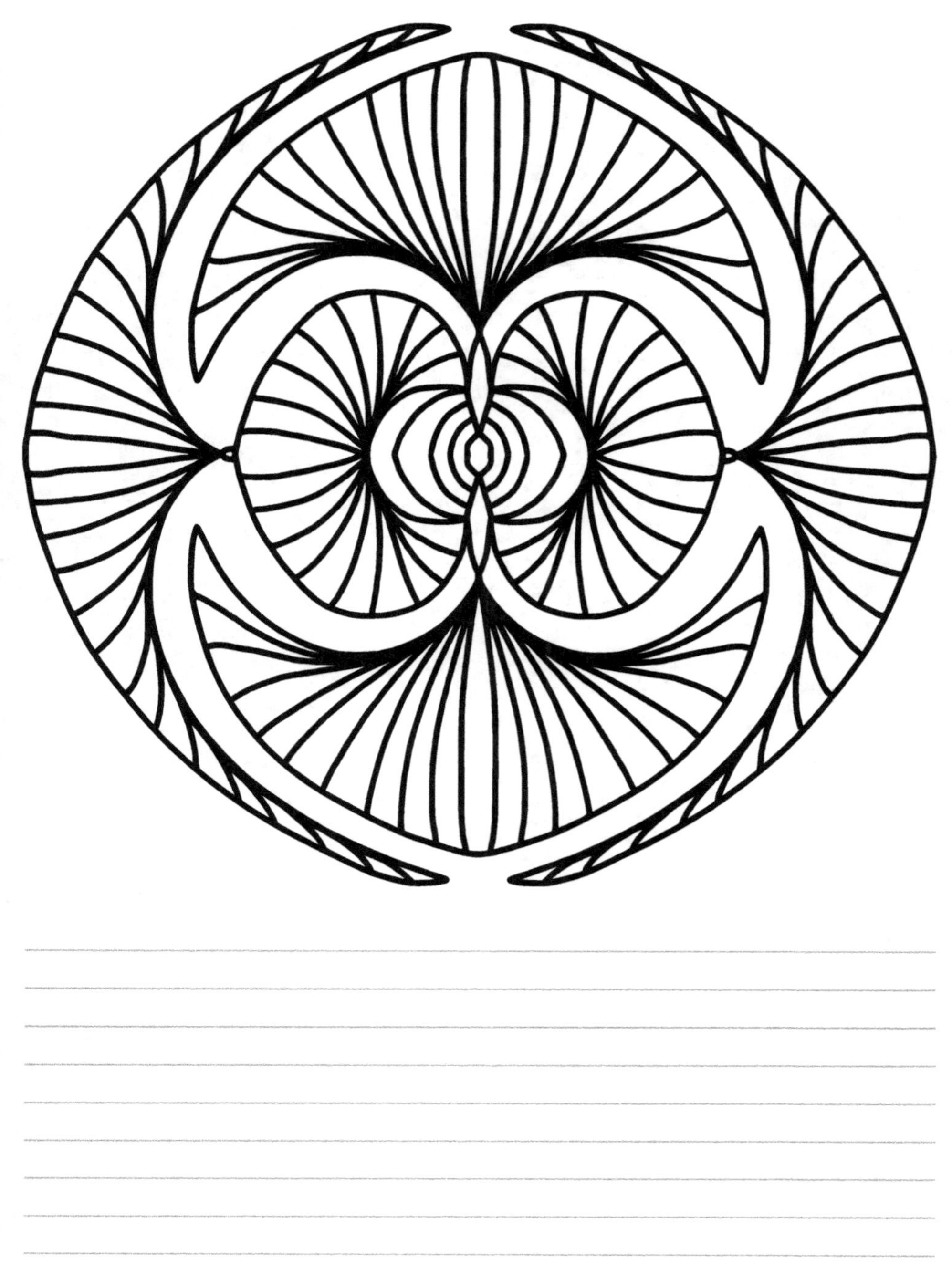

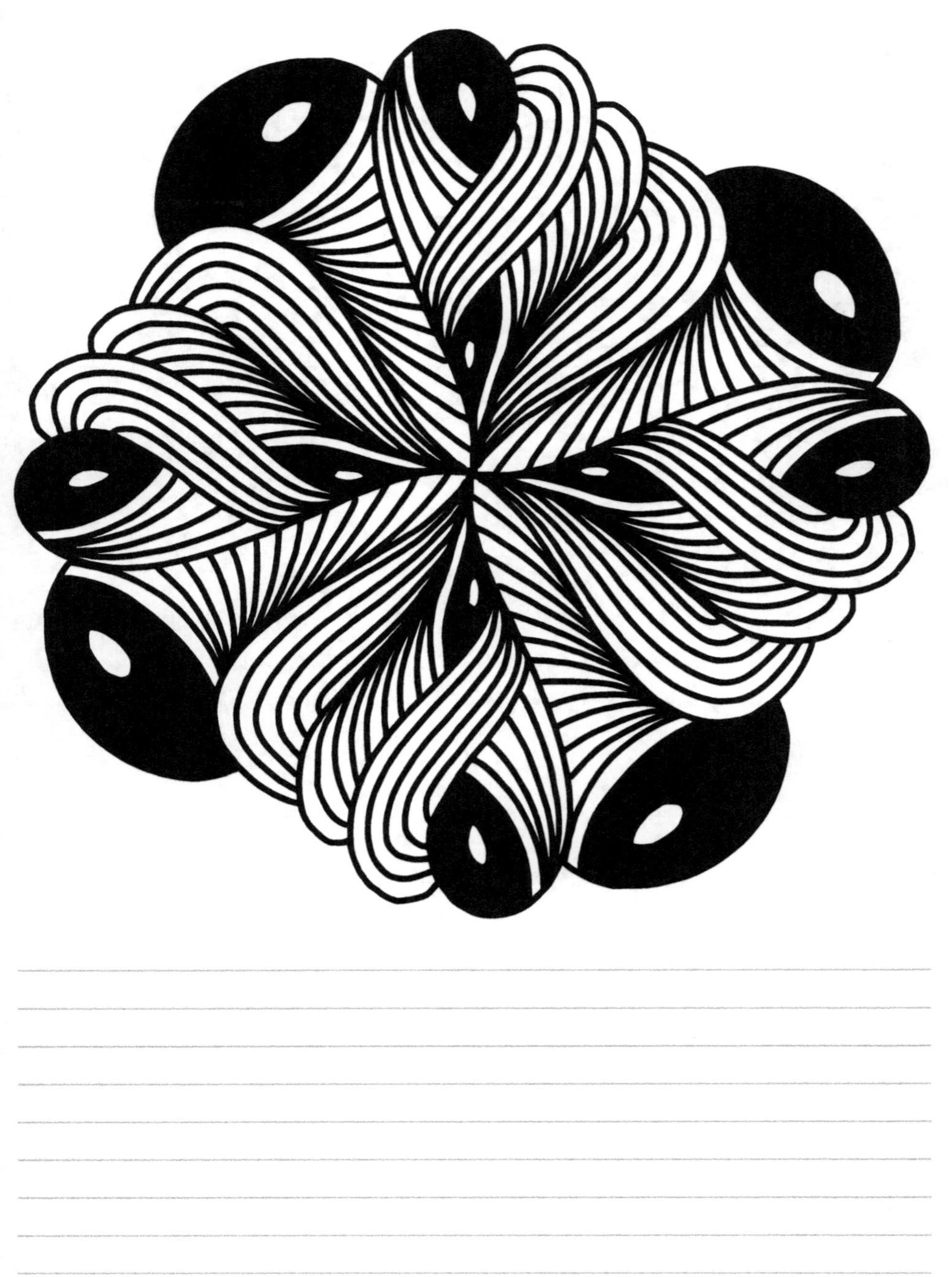

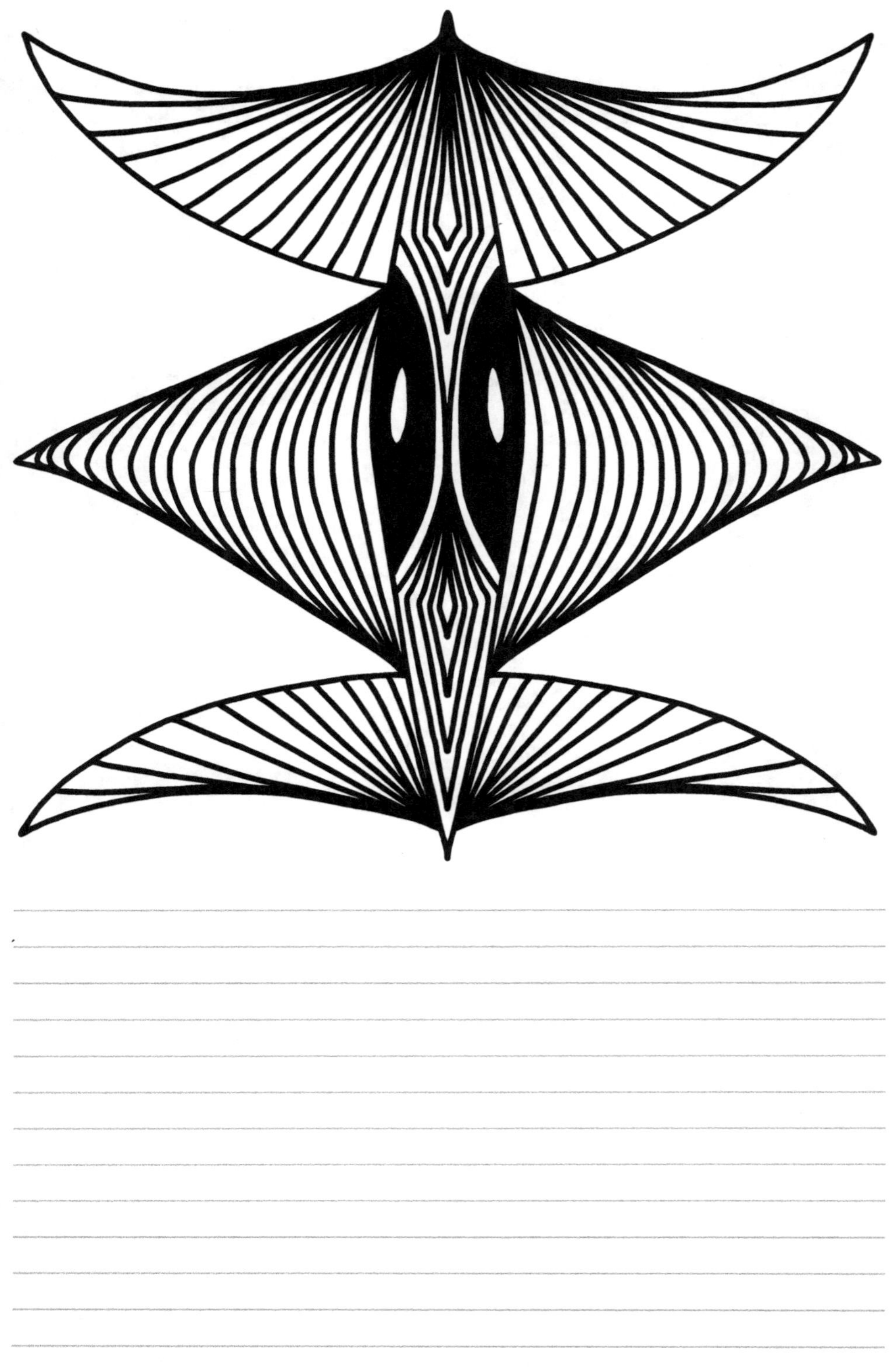

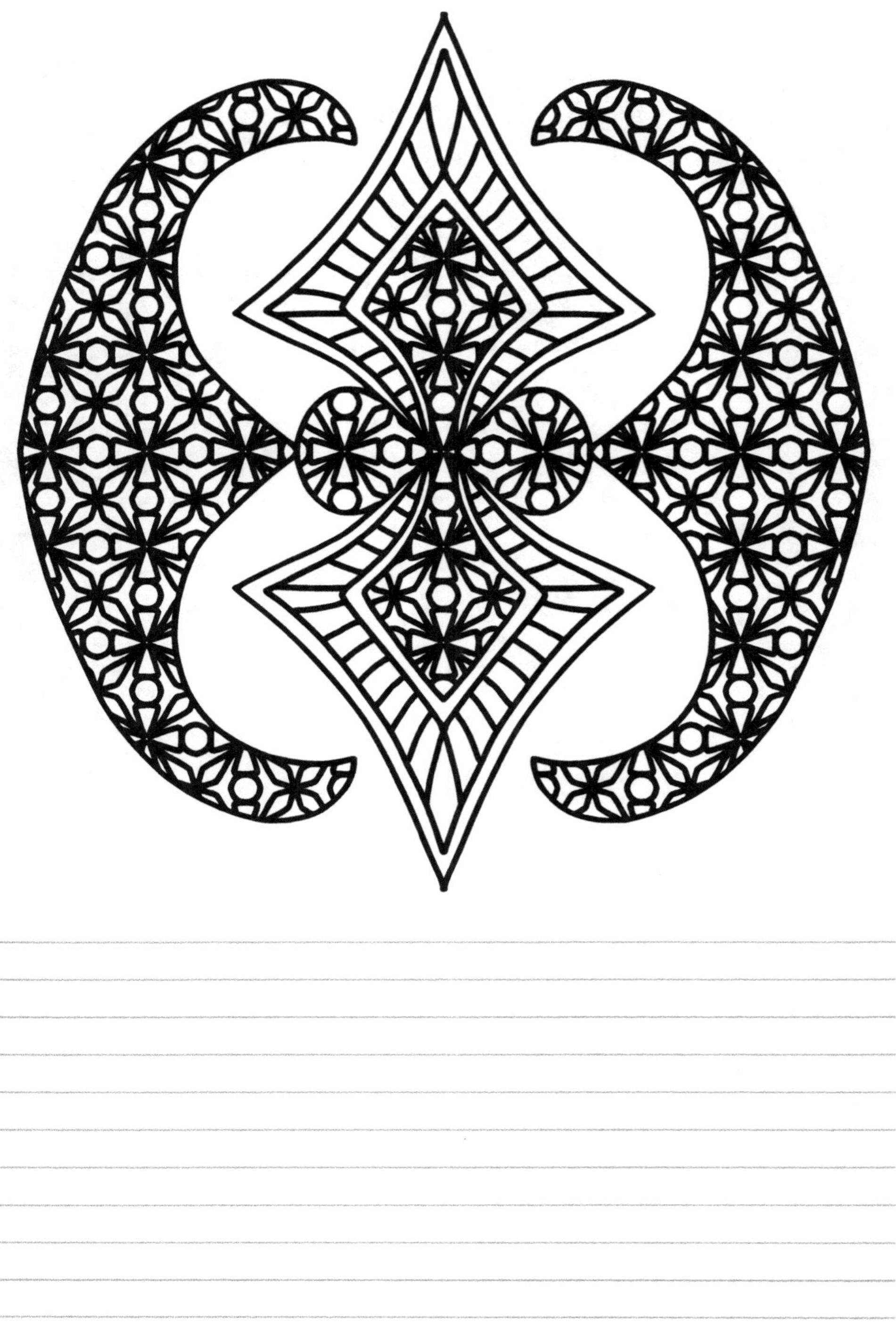

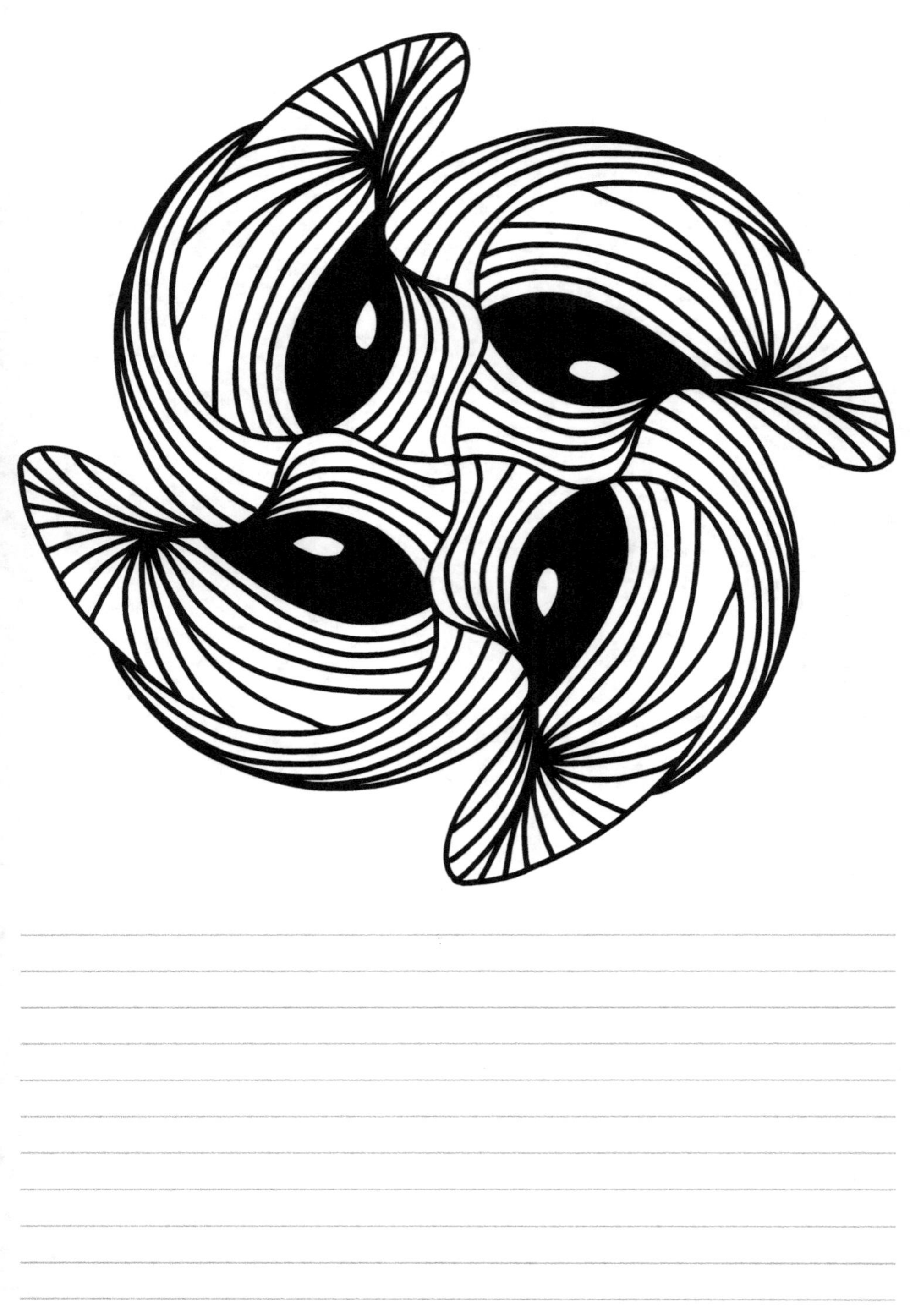

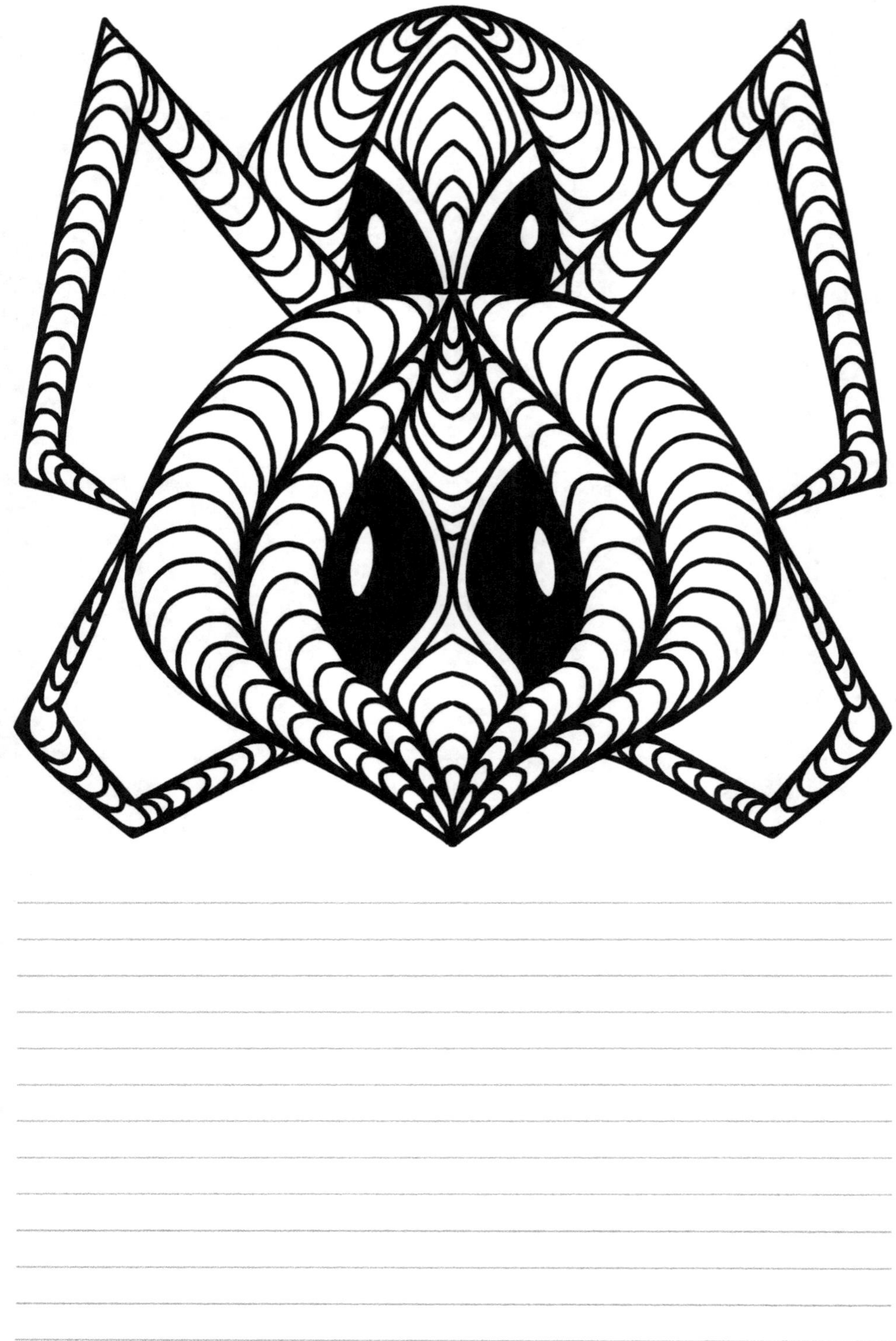

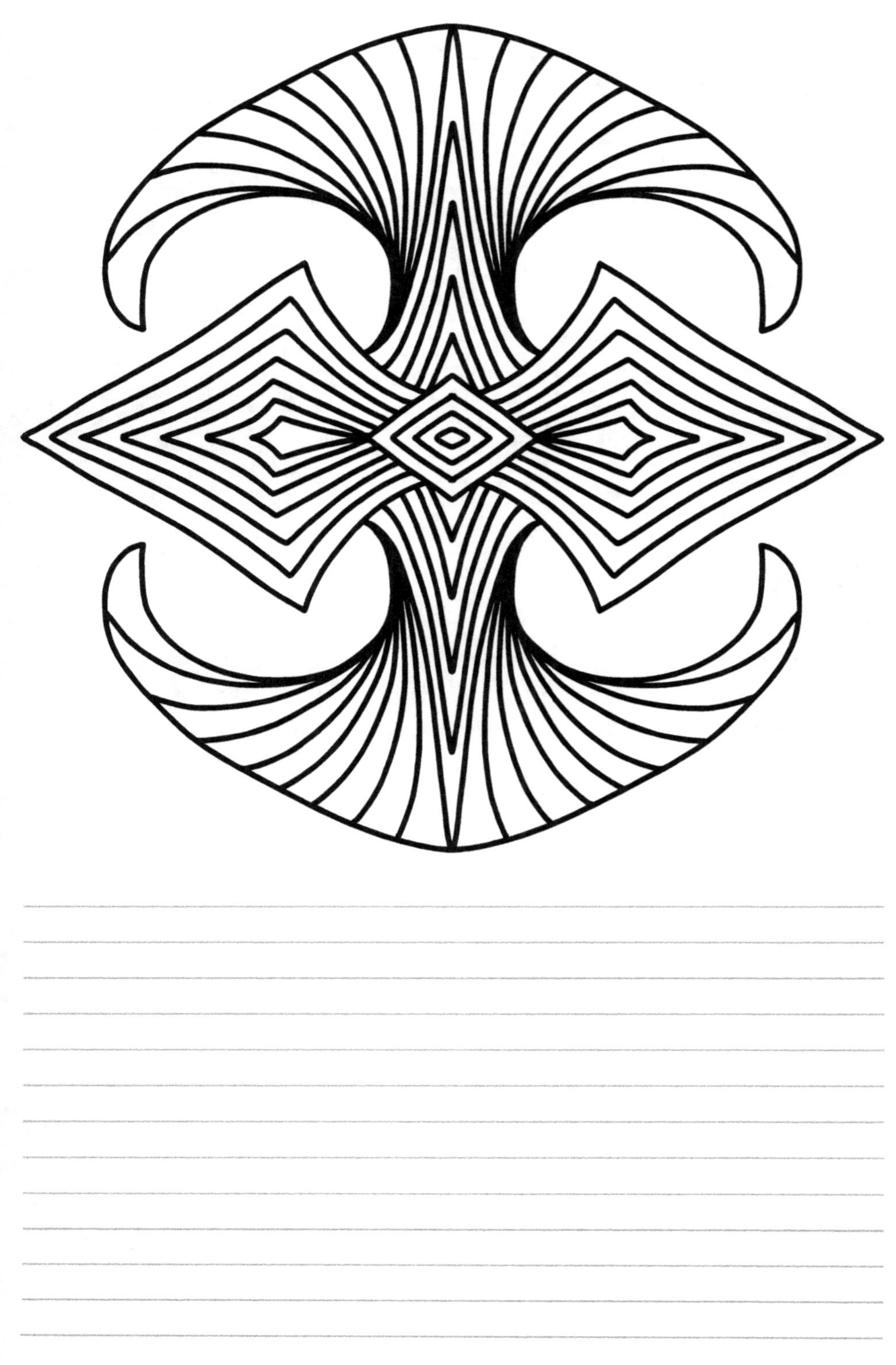

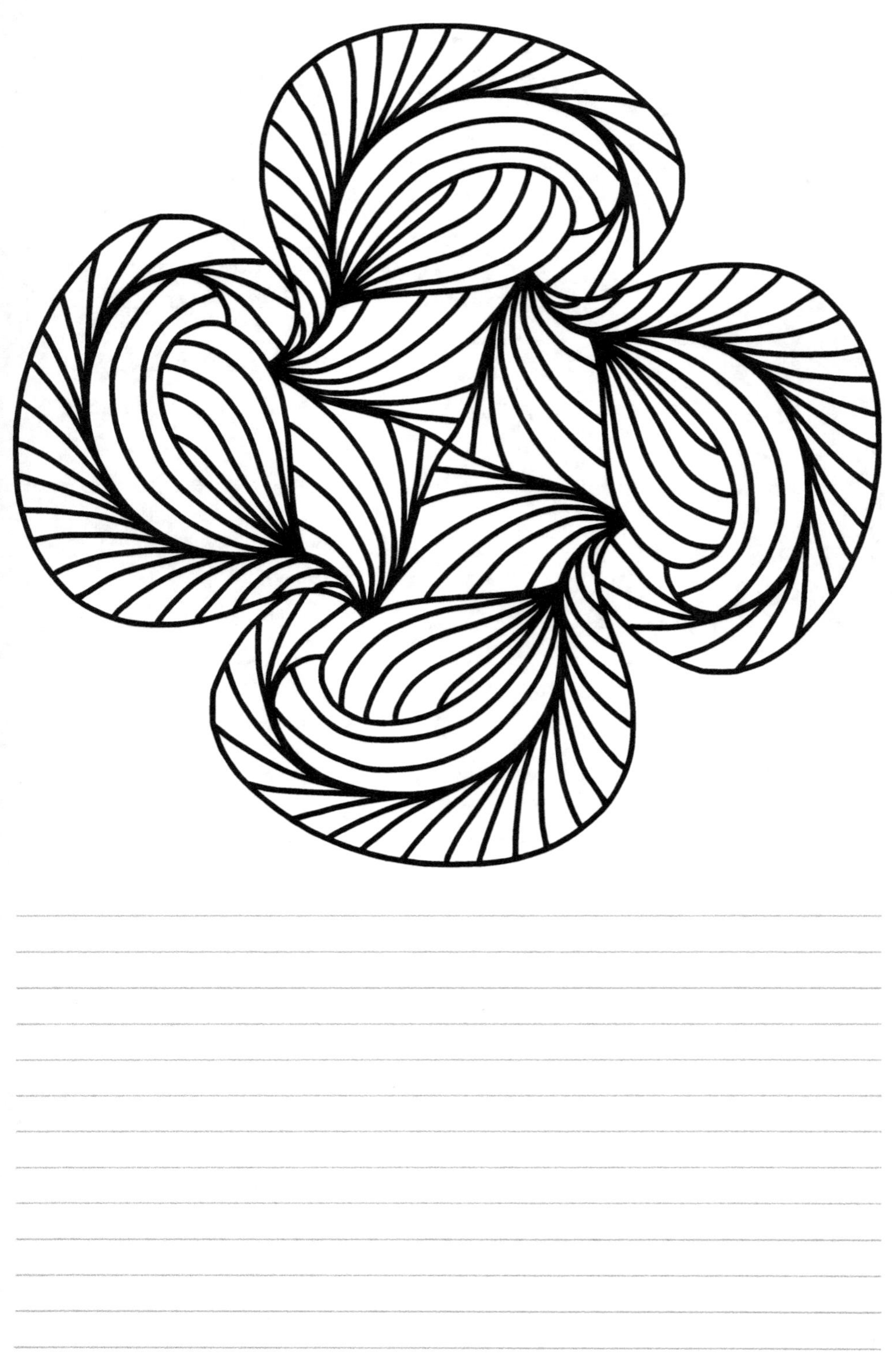

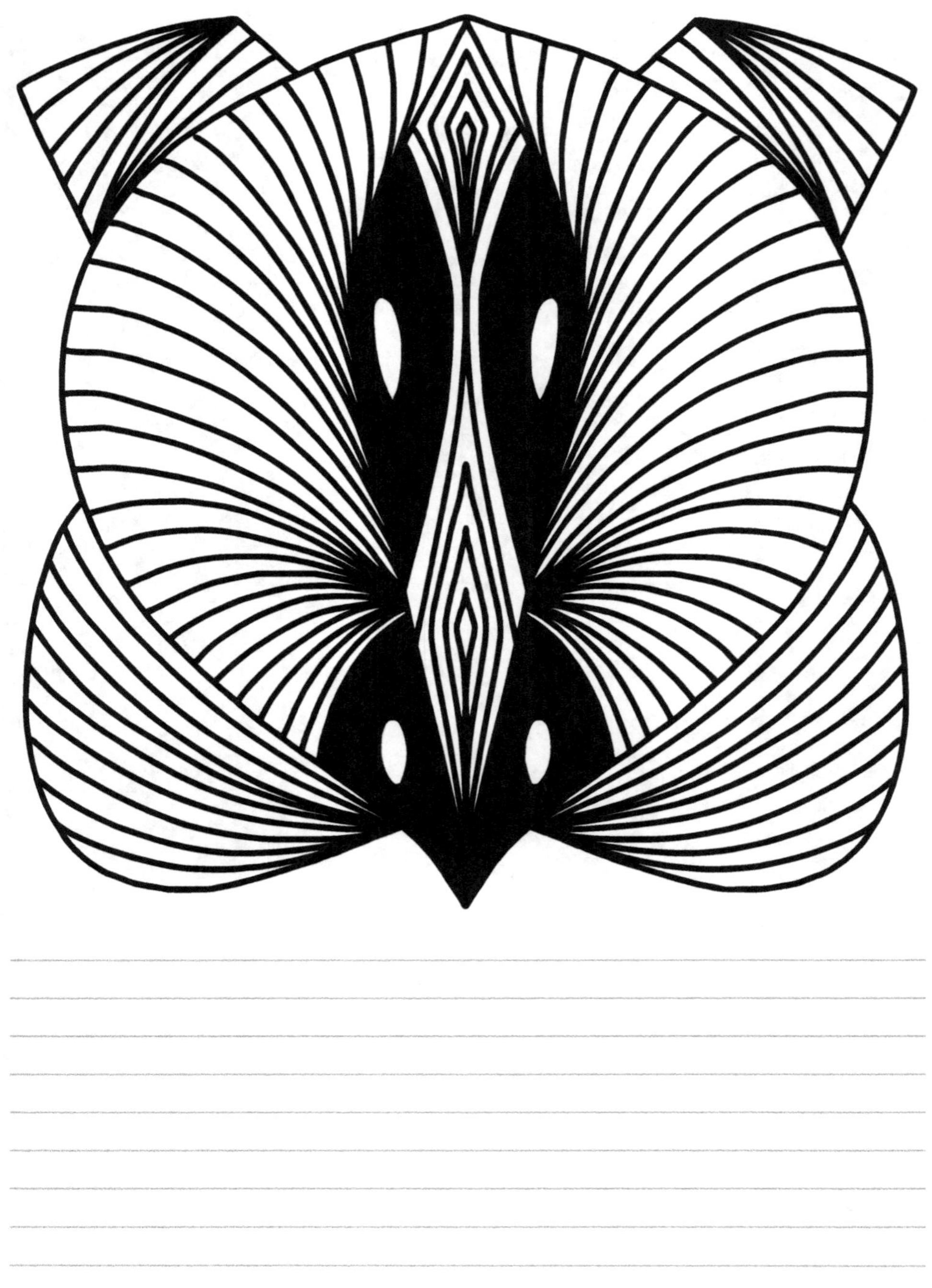

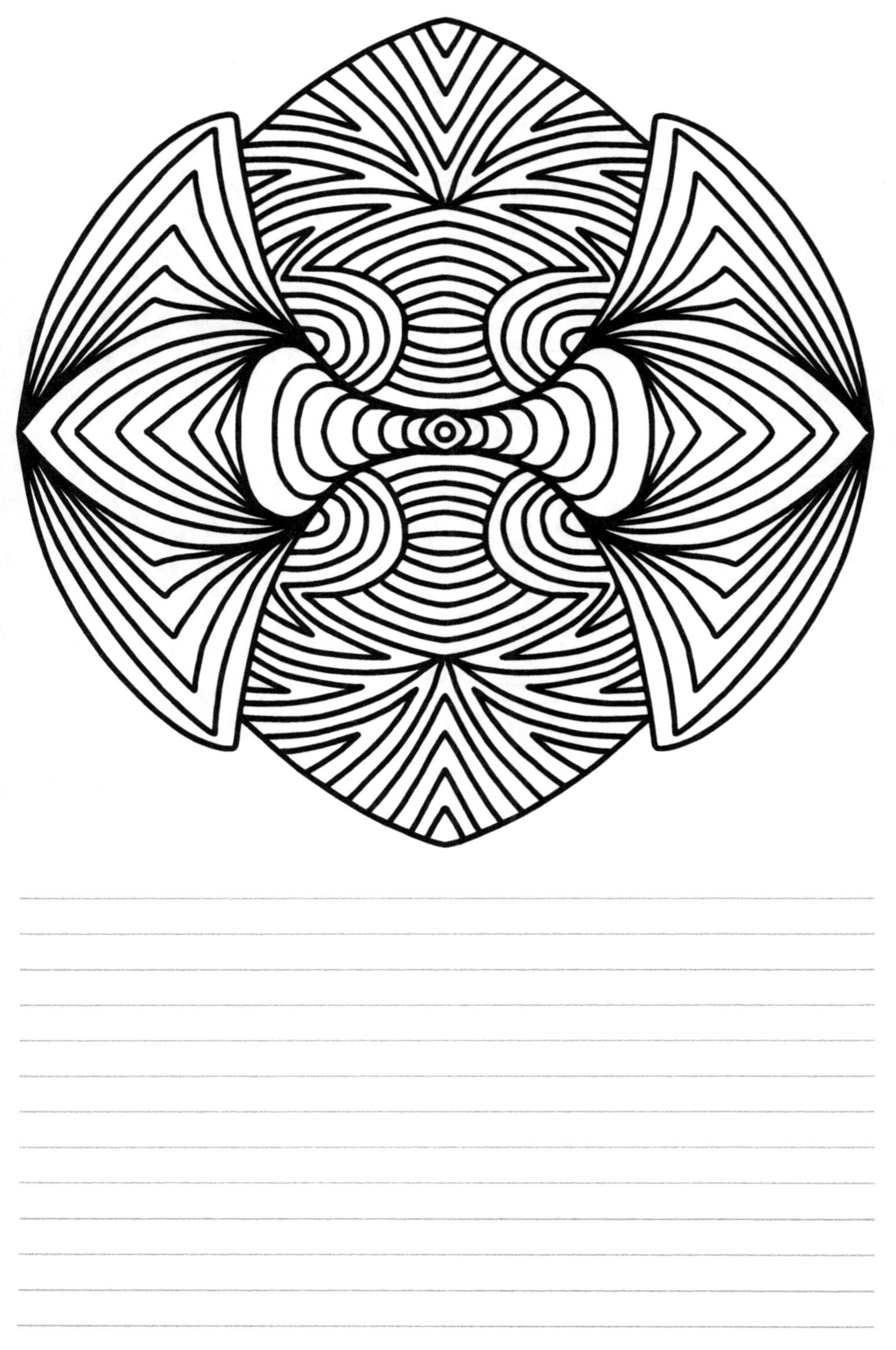

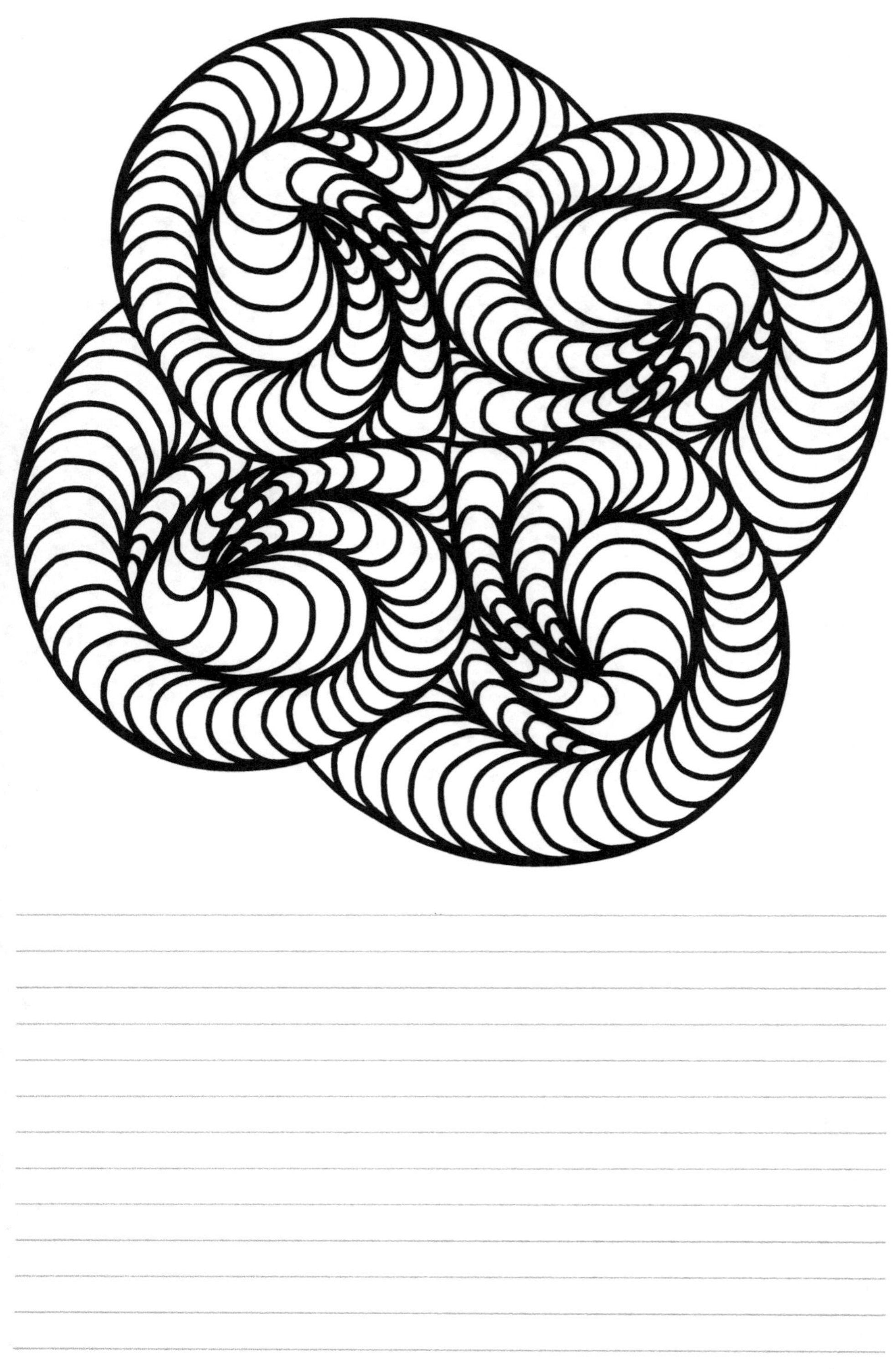

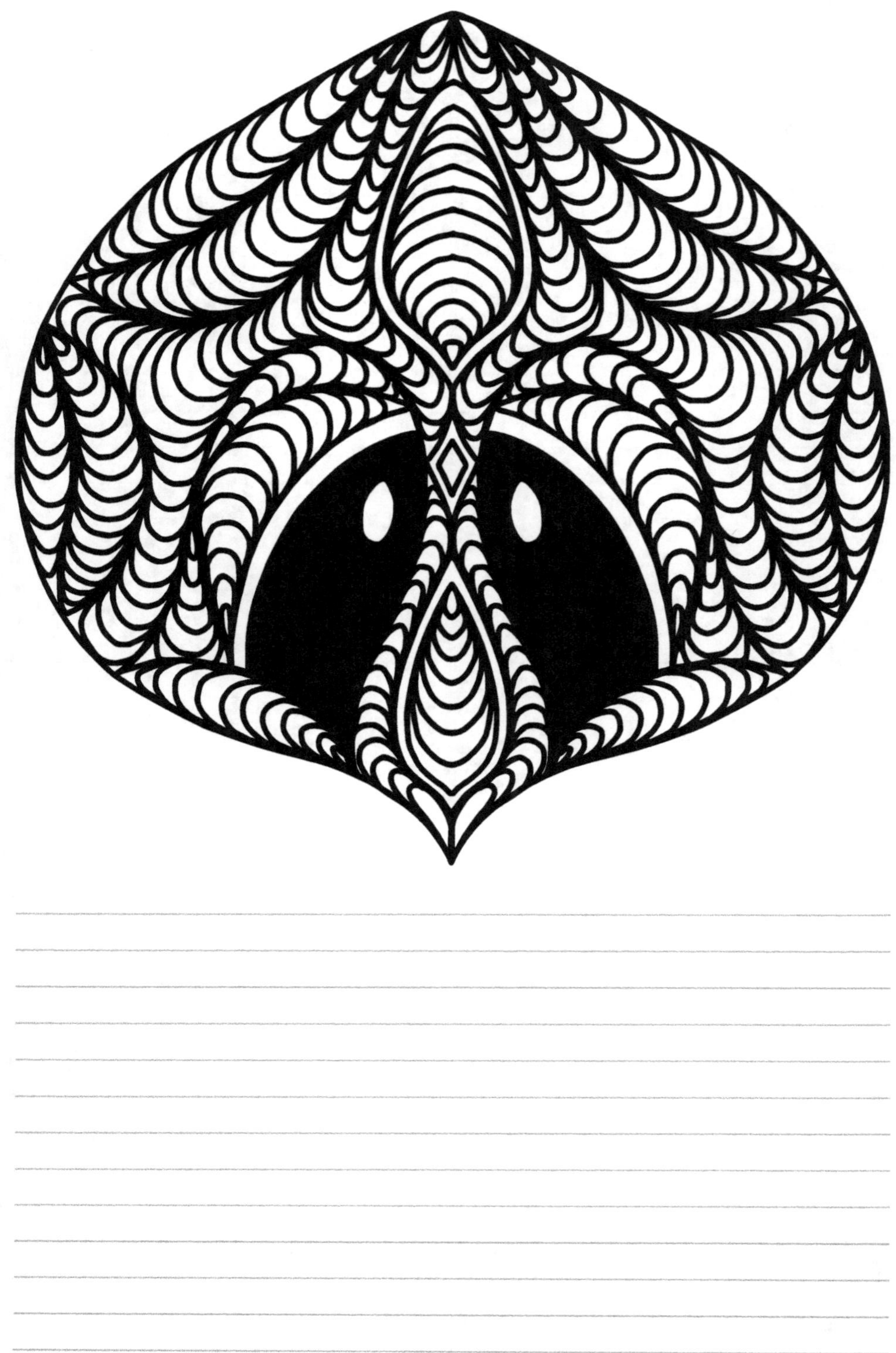

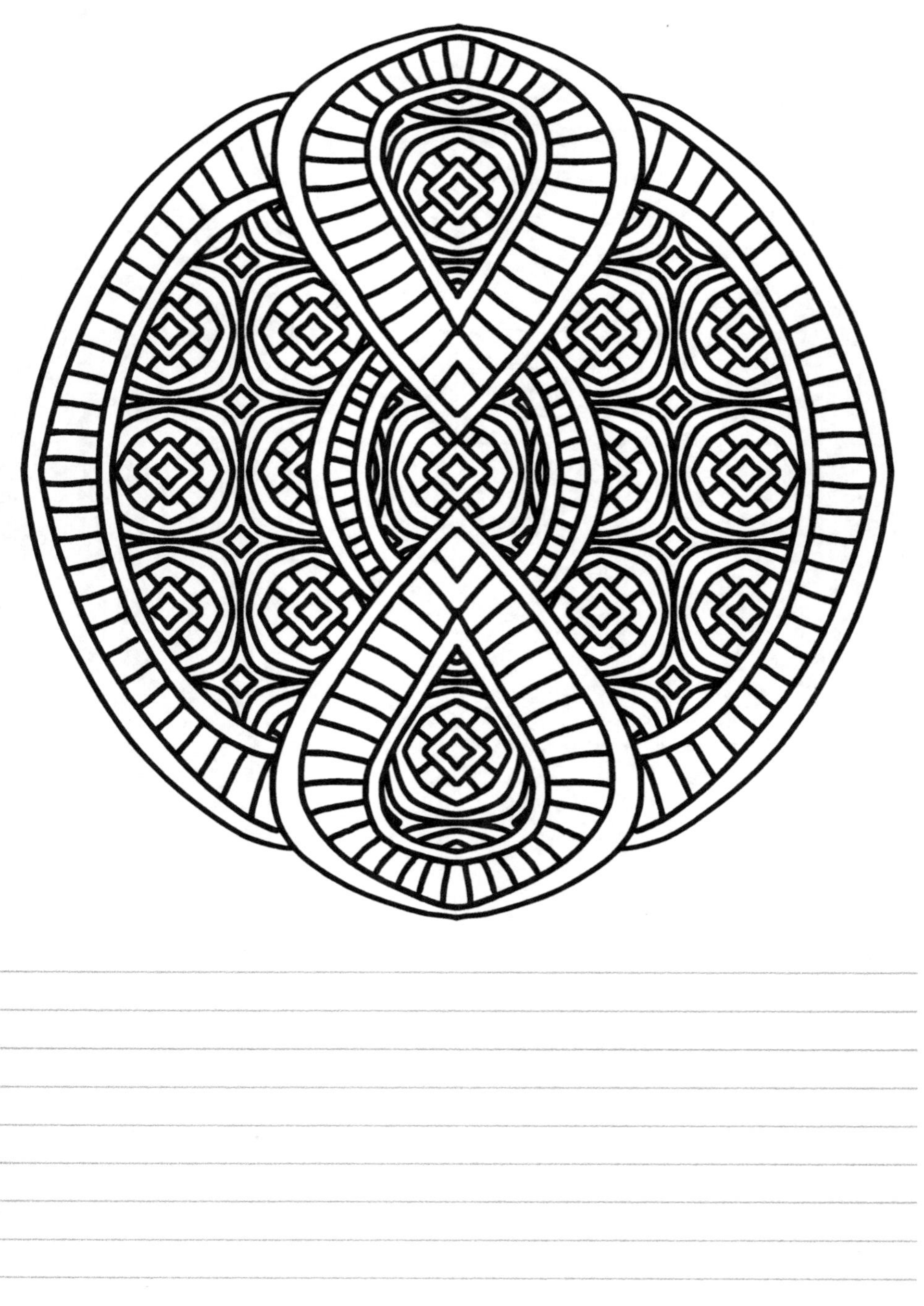

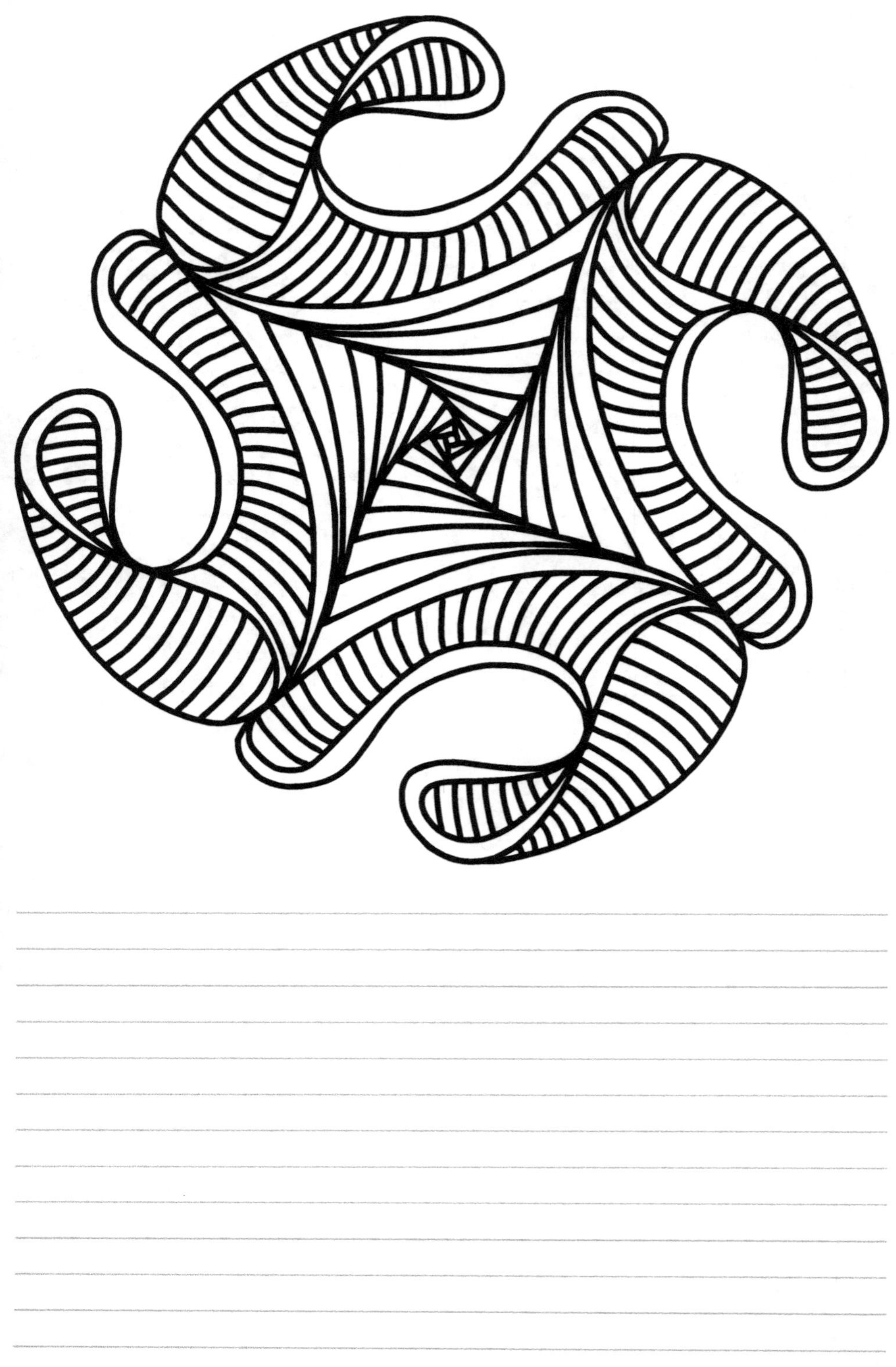

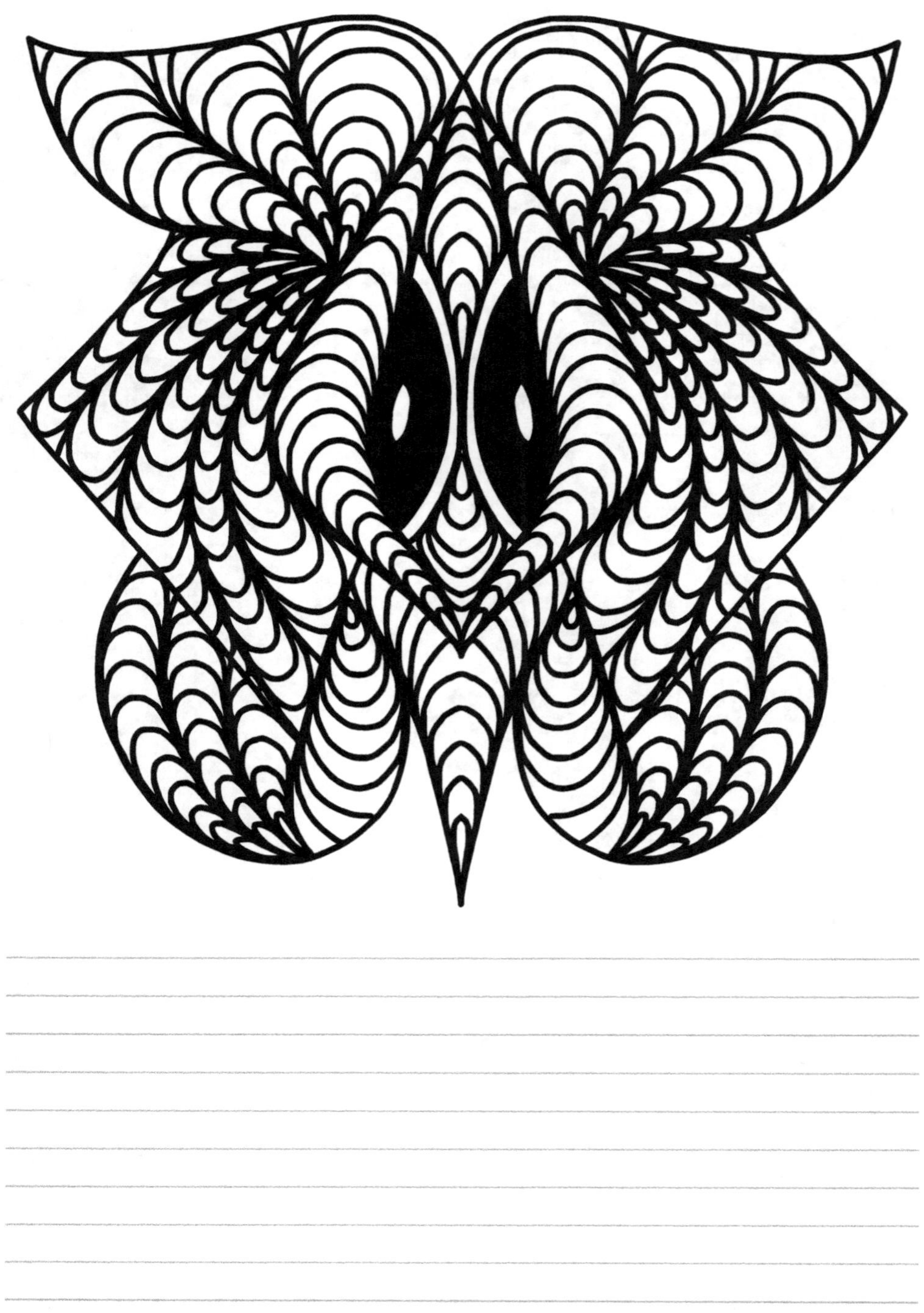

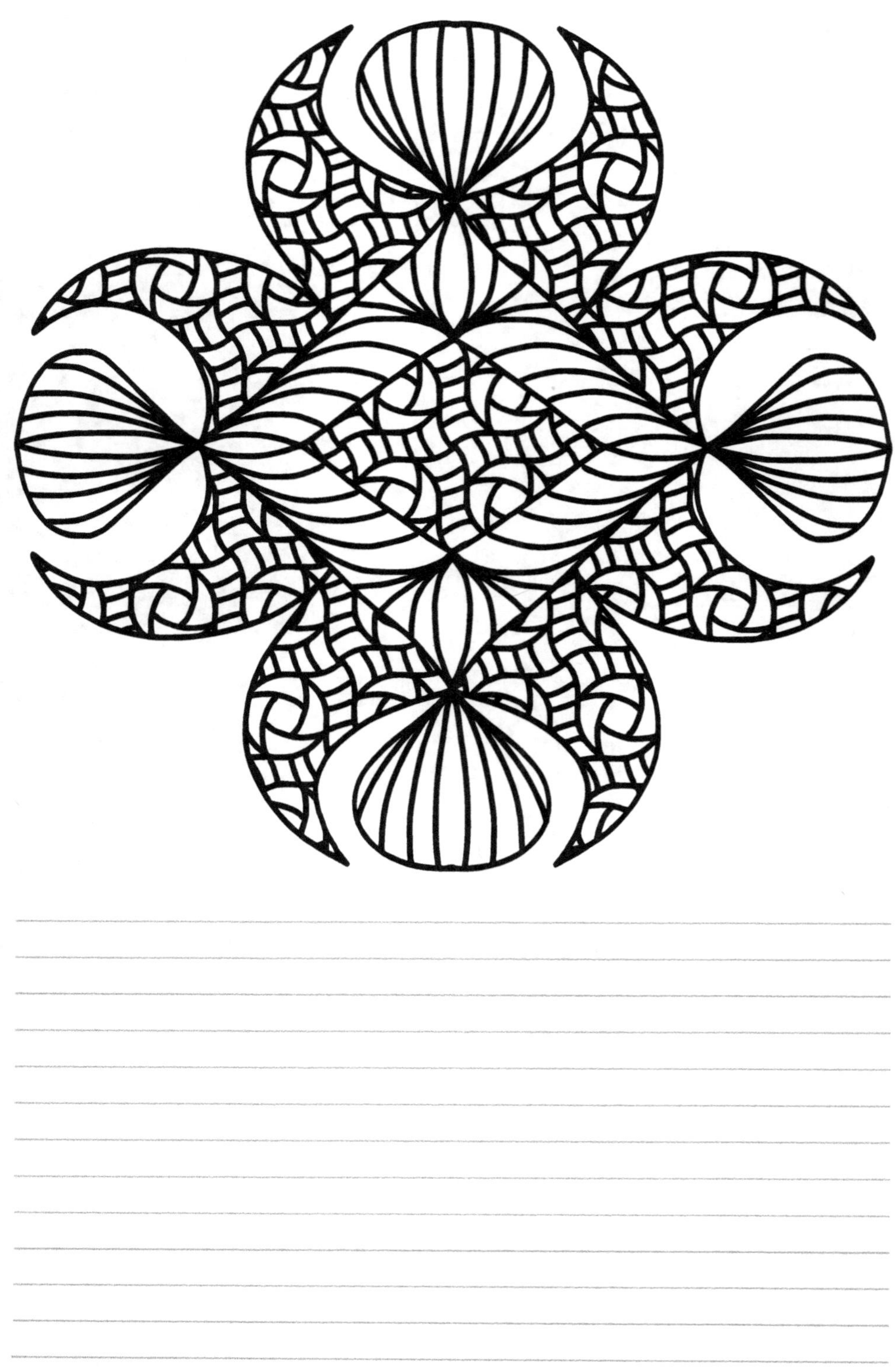

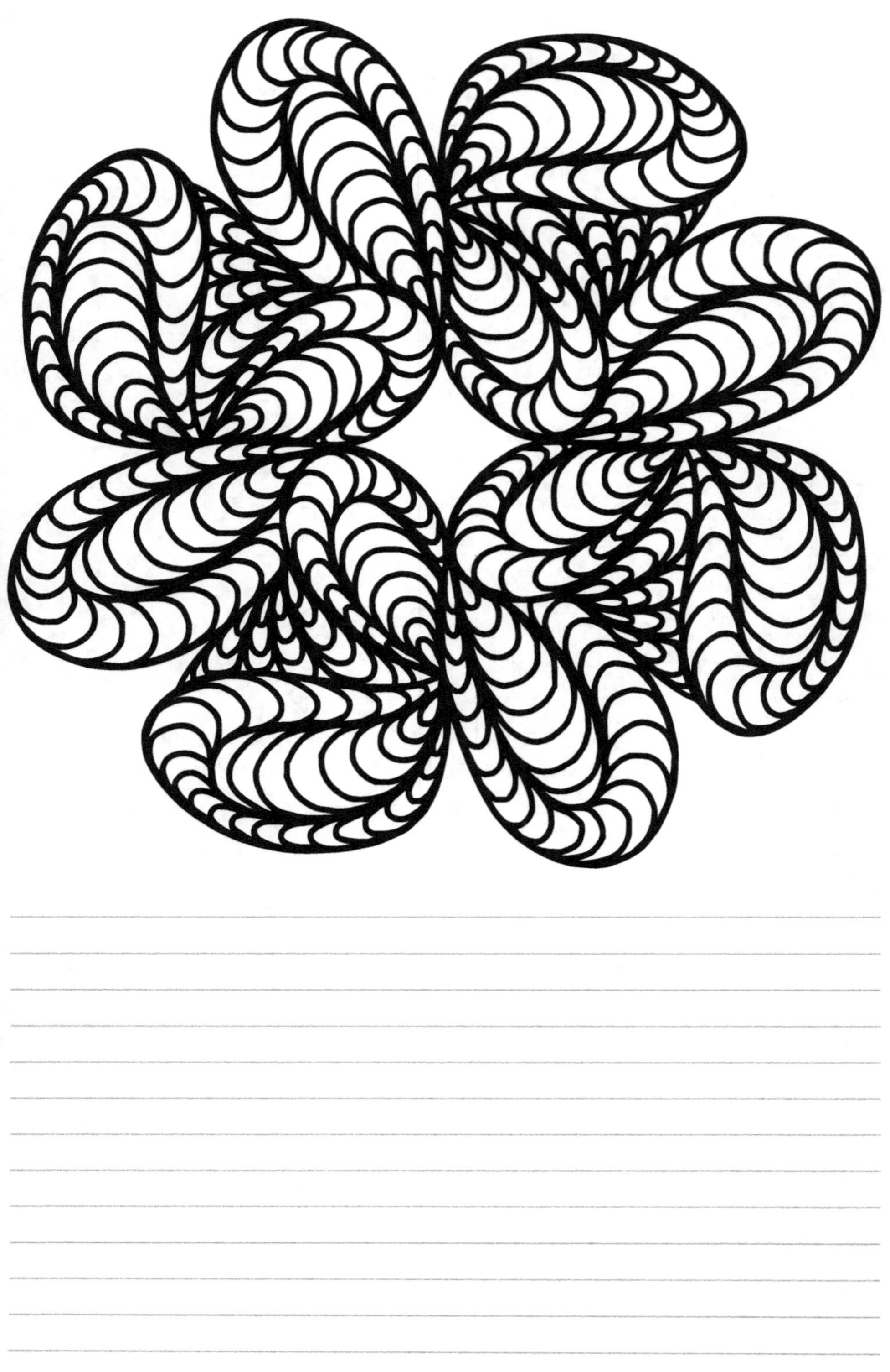

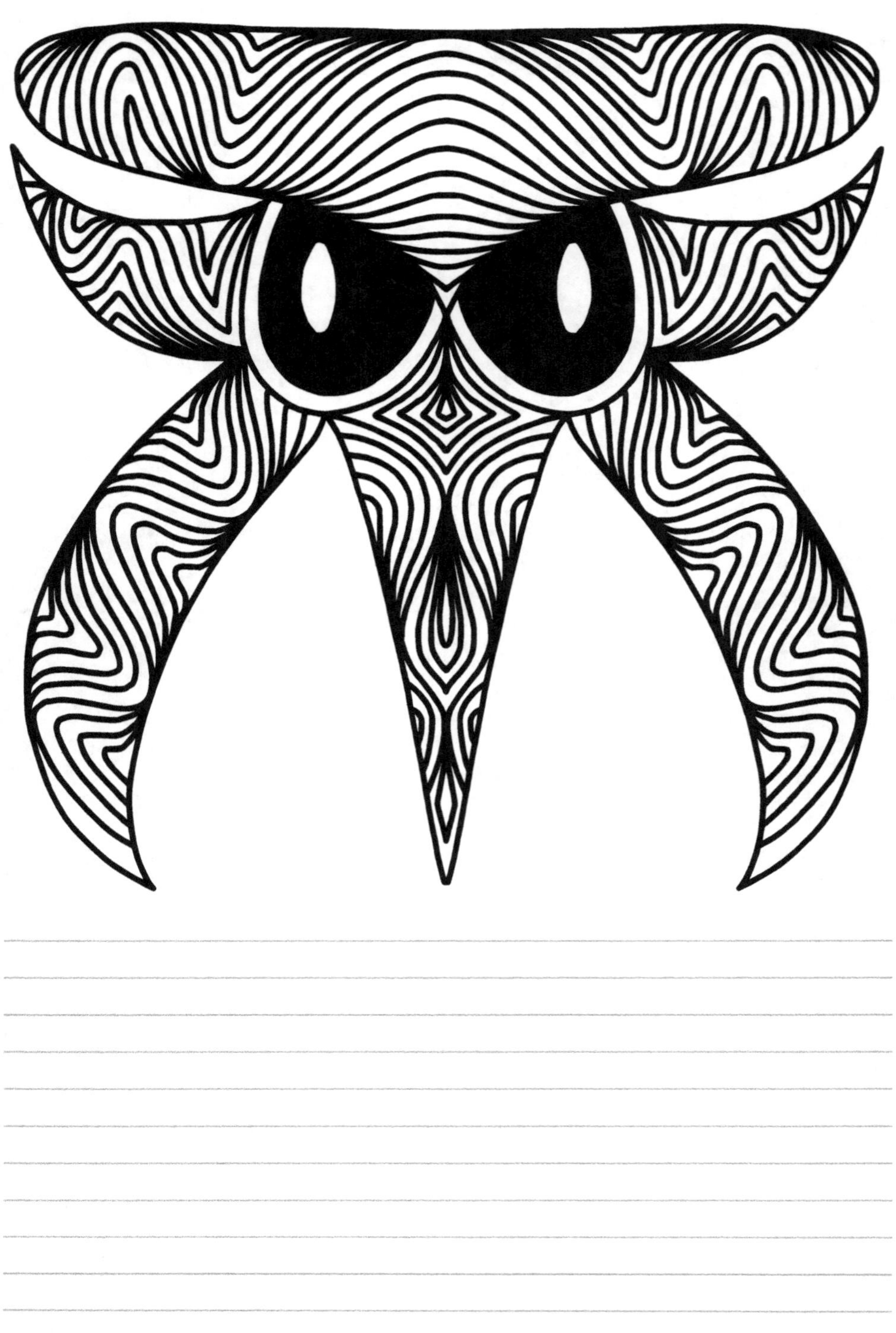

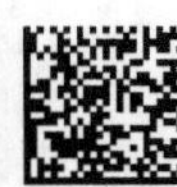

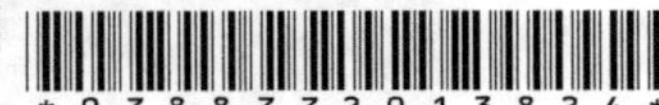
9 788877 201382 4